SELinux Cookbook

Over 70 hands-on recipes to develop fully functional
policies to confine your applications and users
using SELinux

Sven Vermeulen

BIRMINGHAM - MUMBAI

SELinux Cookbook

First published: September 2014

Production reference: 1180914

Published by Packt Publishing Ltd.
Livery Place
35 Livery Street
Birmingham B3 2PB, UK.

ISBN 978-1-78398-966-9

www.packtpub.com

Cover image by Sarath Santhan (sarathsanthan@gmail.com)

Credits

Author
Sven Vermeulen

Reviewers
David Quigley
Sam Wilson
Jason Zaman
Lukáš Zapletal

Commissioning Editor
Usha Iyer

Acquisition Editor
Rebecca Youé

Content Development Editors
Dayan Hyames
Sankalp Pawar

Technical Editor
Mrunal Chavan

Copy Editors
Sayanee Mukherjee
Karuna Narayanan
Laxmi Subramanian

Project Coordinator
Venitha Cutinho

Proofreaders
Simran Bhogal
Paul Hindle

Indexers
Priya Sane
Tejal Soni

Graphics
Valentina D'silva
Disha Haria

Production Coordinators
Kyle Albuquerque
Aparna Bhagat
Komal Ramchandani

Cover Work
Komal Ramchandani

About the Author

Sven Vermeulen is a long-term contributor to various free software projects and the author of various online guides and resources. He got his first taste of free software in 1997 and never looked back. In 2003, he joined the ranks of the Gentoo Linux project as a documentation developer and has since worked in several roles, including Gentoo Foundation trustee, council member, project lead for various documentations, and (his current role) project lead for Gentoo Hardened SELinux integration and the system integrity project.

During this time, Sven gained expertise in several technologies, ranging from operating system level knowledge to application servers. He used his interest in security to guide his projects further in the areas of security guides using SCAP languages, mandatory access controls through SELinux, authentication with PAM, (application) firewalling, and more.

Within SELinux, Sven contributed several policies to the Reference Policy project, and he is actively participating in the policy development and user space development projects.

In his daily job, Sven is an IT infrastructure architect with a European financial institution. The secure implementation of infrastructures (and the surrounding architectural integration) is, of course, an important part of this. Prior to this, he graduated as an MSE in Computer Engineering from Ghent University, and then worked as a web application infrastructure engineer using IBM WebSphere Application Server.

Sven is the main author of *Gentoo Handbook*, which covers the installation and configuration of Gentoo Linux on several architectures. He has also authored the *Linux Sea* online publication, which is a basic introduction to Linux for novice system administrators and *SELinux System Administration*, *Packt Publishing*, which covers SELinux for system administrators.

I would like to dedicate this book to my godfather and friend, Jo Jagers, who suddenly and unexpectedly passed away last year. He showed me the importance of friendship and richness of life. His energetic approach to life is still an example to me.
You will always be missed, my friend.

About the Reviewers

David Quigley started his career as a computer systems researcher for the National Information Assurance Research Lab at the NSA, where he worked as a member of the SELinux team. He led the design and implementation to provide Labeled NFS support for SELinux. He has previously contributed to the open source community by maintaining the Unionfs 1.0 code base and through code contributions to various other projects. He has presented at conferences such as the Ottawa Linux Symposium, the StorageSS workshop, LinuxCon, and several local Linux User Group meetings, where presentation topics included storage, filesystems, and security. David currently works as a Computer Science Professional for the Operations, Analytics, and Software Development (OASD) division at KEYW Corporation, developing innovative system software for Unix and Windows platforms.

> I would like to thank my wonderful wife, Kathy, for all she has done to make sure I have the time to do things such as review this book and travel to give presentations on SELinux. She is the joy of my life and has helped me become the man I am today. I'd also like to thank all my children—Zoe, Jane, and the twins—who remind us to love and cherish the time we have as a family. Also, I thank my parents, Gary and Vicky, for supporting my decisions to change my educational direction and become a computer scientist, allowing me to be where I am today.

Sam Wilson is a systems and security engineer with a focus on Red Hat Enterprise Linux. Having spent 2 years working as an information security consultant and also having passed the Red Hat SELinux Policy Administration exam, he is often asked for SELinux advice within teams he works with. Sam has been active in the GNU/Linux communities since early 2007 and has contributed to NTFreeNet, Darwin Community Arts, Ansible, and the Fedora project. Sam can be found online at `www.cycloptivity.net`.

Jason Zaman is a graduate from Carnegie Mellon University with a degree in Electrical and Computer Engineering. He has been interested in computers and open source and uses Linux from a young age. After using Gentoo Linux for many years, he has now joined the Gentoo Hardened and SELinux projects as a developer. Currently, he works in a start-up company mainly doing Android development and system administration to maintain the servers.

Lukáš Zapletal works as a software engineer in the cloud division of Red Hat, where he develops the Satellite 6.0 product and is also responsible for SELinux policies of the product. He is part of the Fedora, Foreman, Katello, and OpenStack communities. He worked as an Editor in Chief at Linux+ and cofounded the *LinuxEXPRES (Czech)* magazine.

Red Hat is the world's leading provider of open source solutions, using a community-powered approach to provide reliable and high-performing cloud, virtualization, storage, Linux, and middleware technologies.

I'd like to thank Mirek Grepl and Dan Walsh from the Red Hat SELinux team for all their answers, and my family, Broňa and Ondra, for allowing me to review this amazing book.

www.PacktPub.com

Support files, eBooks, discount offers, and more

You might want to visit www.PacktPub.com for support files and downloads related to your book.

Did you know that Packt offers eBook versions of every book published, with PDF and ePub files available? You can upgrade to the eBook version at www.PacktPub.com and as a print book customer, you are entitled to a discount on the eBook copy. Get in touch with us at service@packtpub.com for more details.

At www.PacktPub.com, you can also read a collection of free technical articles, sign up for a range of free newsletters and receive exclusive discounts and offers on Packt books and eBooks.

http://PacktLib.PacktPub.com

Do you need instant solutions to your IT questions? PacktLib is Packt's online digital book library. Here, you can access, read and search across Packt's entire library of books.

Why subscribe?

- ▸ Fully searchable across every book published by Packt
- ▸ Copy and paste, print and bookmark content
- ▸ On demand and accessible via web browser

Free access for Packt account holders

If you have an account with Packt at www.PacktPub.com, you can use this to access PacktLib today and view nine entirely free books. Simply use your login credentials for immediate access.

Table of Contents

Preface

SELinux can be seen as a daunting beast to tame. For many, it is considered to be a complex security system on the already versatile environment that Linux can be. But as with most IT-related services, it is the unfamiliarity with the technology that is causing the notion of having a complicated system.

It is, however, nothing like that. SELinux is not all that difficult to understand. If it were, then Linux distributions such as Red Hat Enterprise Linux wouldn't enable it by default.

To support everyone in their daily operations with SELinux-enabled systems, this book came to life. It contains numerous chapters on the various aspects of SELinux handling and policy development in a recipe-based approach that allows every person to quickly dive into the details and challenges that making a system more secure brings forth.

What this will not present are administration-related commands and examples. For that, I have written another better-suited SELinux resource, *SELinux System Administration*, *Packt Publishing*, which covers the system administration tasks of SELinux-enabled systems, such as dealing with SELinux Booleans and file context changes as well as an introduction to the SELinux technology.

This book is also not a reference for the SELinux policy language in all its glory. Although the most common statements will be mentioned and used several times, it should be noted that the SELinux policy language and its internal architecture has a much wider scope. For a good language and component reference, *The SELinux Notebook – The Foundations*, *Richard Haines*, is recommended. This resource is available online at http://www.freetechbooks.com/the-selinux-notebook-the-foundations-t785.html.

What this book covers

Chapter 1, The SELinux Development Environment, tells us how to set up the SELinux policy development environment through which further policy development can occur. We will look into a structured, reusable method for SELinux policy development and will create our first set of SELinux policy modules that are nicely integrated with the existing SELinux policies.

Chapter 2, Dealing with File Labels, focuses on how file labels are set and managed. We will learn how to configure the SELinux policy ourselves as well as how to use and declare file contexts and assign the right context to the right type of resource.

Chapter 3, Confining Web Applications, covers the default confinement of the web server SELinux domain and explains how to enhance the existing policy to suit our needs. Additional SELinux support through the mod_selinux Apache module is also covered.

Chapter 4, Creating a Desktop Application Policy, is the first chapter where an entirely new application domain and policy is written. We will look at how the policy needs to be structured and the policy rules that are needed in order to successfully and securely run the application.

Chapter 5, Creating a Server Policy, follows the previous chapter's momentum but now with a focus on server services. This chapter targets the differences between desktop application policies and server policies, and we will develop a fully functioning SELinux policy module together with the necessary administrative policy interfaces needed to integrate the policy in a larger SELinux environment.

Chapter 6, Setting Up Separate Roles, looks into the role-based access controls that SELinux offers. We create our own set of roles with the least privilege principle in mind. After considering the definition of SELinux users and roles, we then practice the management of these roles in larger environments.

Chapter 7, Choosing the Confinement Level, inspects the different confinement levels that policies can use and how these are implemented on the system. We learn about the pros and cons of each confinement level and create our own policy set that provides the different levels.

Chapter 8, Debugging SELinux, scrutinizes the various methods available to debug SELinux behavior and policies. We acquire the necessary skills to work with the Linux auditing subsystem to generate additional logging and perform advanced queries against the SELinux policy. In this chapter, we also uncover why certain popular Linux debugging tools do not (properly) work on an SELinux-enabled system.

Chapter 9, Aligning SELinux with DAC, examines how SELinux can be used to enhance the existing Linux DAC restrictions. We deal with the various technologies available and how the SELinux policy can be augmented to work properly with those technologies.

Chapter 10, Handling SELinux-aware Applications, considers the SELinux-aware applications and the interaction (and debugging difficulties) they have with the system and SELinux in general. We learn how to configure these applications' SELinux integration and how to debug the applications when things go wrong. This chapter also describes how to create our own SELinux-aware application.

What you need for this book

As the book focuses on hands-on experience, it is seriously recommended to have an SELinux-enabled system at your disposal. Many distributions offer live environments that can be used to perform initial investigations with, but ensure that you pick one that can persist the changes made to the system.

An SELinux-enabled system should be using a recent set of SELinux libraries and user space utilities. This book is written based on Gentoo Hardened, running the SELinux user space libraries and utilities released in October 2013 (such as libselinux-2.2.2) with the reference policy released in March 2014. The distribution itself is not that important, as everything in this book is distribution-independent, so it is well usable for Fedora and Red Hat Enterprise Linux, although the latter—at the time of writing, Version 6—is still using older versions of the SELinux user space libraries and utilities.

From an experience point of view, you should be well-versed in Linux system administration as SELinux policy development and integration requires good knowledge of the components that we are about to confine and protect. This book assumes that you are familiar with the Git version control system as an end user. This book also assumes basic knowledge of how SELinux works on a system.

Who this book is for

This book is meant for Linux system administrators and security administrators who want to perform the following tasks:

- ▸ Fine-tune the SELinux subsystem on their Linux systems
- ▸ Develop SELinux policies for applications and users
- ▸ Tightly integrate SELinux within their current processes

Conventions

In this book, you will find a number of styles of text that distinguish between different kinds of information. Here are some examples of these styles, and an explanation of their meaning.

Code words in text, database table names, folder names, filenames, file extensions, pathnames, dummy URLs, user input, and Twitter handles are shown as follows: "Using the `auditallow` statement, we can track SELinux policy decisions and assist in the development of policies and debugging of application behavior."

A block of code is set as follows:

```
write_files_pattern(syslogd_t, named_conf_t, named_conf_t)
allow syslogd_t named_conf_t:file setattr_file_perms;
```

When we wish to draw your attention to a particular part of a code block, the relevant lines or items are set in bold:

```
policy_module(mysysadm, 0.1)
gen_require(`
  type sysadm_t;
')
logging_exec_syslog(sysadm_t)
```

Any command-line input or output is written as follows:

```
~# setsebool cron_userdomain_transition on
~# grep crond_t /etc/selinux/mcs/contexts/users/user_u
system_r:crond_t   user_r:user_t
```

New terms and **important words** are shown in bold. Words that you see on the screen, in menus or dialog boxes for example, appear in the text like this: "Capabilities are well explained on Chris Friedhoff's **POSIX Capabilities & File POSIX Capabilities** page."

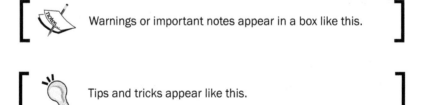

Warnings or important notes appear in a box like this.

Tips and tricks appear like this.

Reader feedback

Feedback from our readers is always welcome. Let us know what you think about this book—what you liked or may have disliked. Reader feedback is important for us to develop titles that you really get the most out of.

To send us general feedback, simply send an e-mail to feedback@packtpub.com, and mention the book title through the subject of your message.

If there is a topic that you have expertise in and you are interested in either writing or contributing to a book, see our author guide on www.packtpub.com/authors.

Customer support

Now that you are the proud owner of a Packt book, we have a number of things to help you to get the most from your purchase.

Downloading the example code

You can download the example code files for all Packt books you have purchased from your account at http://www.packtpub.com. If you purchased this book elsewhere, you can visit http://www.packtpub.com/support and register to have the files e-mailed directly to you.

Errata

Although we have taken every care to ensure the accuracy of our content, mistakes do happen. If you find a mistake in one of our books—maybe a mistake in the text or the code—we would be grateful if you would report this to us. By doing so, you can save other readers from frustration and help us improve subsequent versions of this book. If you find any errata, please report them by visiting http://www.packtpub.com/support, selecting your book, clicking on the **errata submission form** link, and entering the details of your errata. Once your errata are verified, your submission will be accepted and the errata will be uploaded to our website, or added to any list of existing errata, under the Errata section of that title.

Piracy

Piracy of copyright material on the Internet is an ongoing problem across all media. At Packt, we take the protection of our copyright and licenses very seriously. If you come across any illegal copies of our works, in any form, on the Internet, please provide us with the location address or website name immediately so that we can pursue a remedy.

Please contact us at copyright@packtpub.com with a link to the suspected pirated material.

We appreciate your help in protecting our authors, and our ability to bring you valuable content.

Questions

You can contact us at questions@packtpub.com if you are having a problem with any aspect of the book, and we will do our best to address it.

1

The SELinux Development Environment

This chapter covers the setup of the SELinux policy development environment. We will cover the following topics in this chapter:

- ▶ Creating the development environment
- ▶ Building a simple SELinux module
- ▶ Calling refpolicy interfaces
- ▶ Creating our own interface
- ▶ Using the refpolicy naming convention
- ▶ Distributing SELinux policy modules

Introduction

Similar to any other software development, having a well-functioning development environment is essential to successfully create and manage SELinux policies. Such an environment should not only support version control, but also be able to quickly search through the sources or show definitions.

With SELinux, this means that the policy module sources (which are all readable text files) should be stored in a structured manner, the upstream project that provides SELinux policies should be readily accessible, and the necessary functions or scripts to query and search through the policies should be available.

Adventurous users might want to take a look at the **SELinux Policy IDE** (**SLIDE**) as offered by Tresys Technology (`http://oss.tresys.com/projects/slide`). In this book, we do not focus on this IDE; instead, we use whatever file editor the user wants (such as VIM, Emacs, or Kate) and enhance the environment through the necessary shell functions and commands.

Before we cover the setup of the development environment, let's do a quick recapitulation of what SELinux is.

About SELinux

The **Security Enhanced Linux** (**SELinux**) project is the result of projects initiated and supported by the US **National Security Agency** (**NSA**) and came to life in December 2000. It is the implementation of a security system architecture with a flexible, policy-driven configuration approach. This architecture is called the **Flux Advanced Security Kernel** (**Flask**), and its related resources are still an important read for everyone involved with SELinux.

Most papers are linked through the Flask website at `http://www.cs.utah.edu/flux/ fluke/html/flask.html`. The following are some examples of these papers:

> ▸ The paper called *The Inevitability of Failure: The Flawed Assumption of Security in Modern Computing Environments* is still a very topical paper on why mandatory access controls are needed in operating systems

> ▸ The NSA publication, *Implementing SELinux as a Linux Security Module*, available at `http://www.nsa.gov/research/_files/publications/ implementing_selinux.pdf`, goes deeper into how SELinux is implemented

Nowadays, SELinux can be best seen as an additional layer of security services on top of the existing Linux operating system. It is part of the mainstream Linux kernel and uses the **Linux Security Modules** (**LSM**) interfaces to hook into the interaction between processes (user space) and resources. It manages various access services (such as the reading of files, getting directory attributes, binding to domain sockets, connecting to TCP sockets, and gaining additional capabilities) through a powerful approach called **type enforcement**.

The following diagram displays the high-level functional position of the SELinux subsystem. Whenever a subject (in the drawing, this is the **Application**) wants to perform an action against a resource, this action is first checked by the Discretionary Access Control mechanism that the Linux kernel provides. After the action is checked and allowed by the DAC mechanism, the LSM implementation (against which SELinux is registered) calls the hooks that the SELinux subsystem has provided. SELinux then checks the policy (through the cache, and if the access is not registered in the cache yet, it checks in the entire policy) and returns whether the access should be allowed or not.

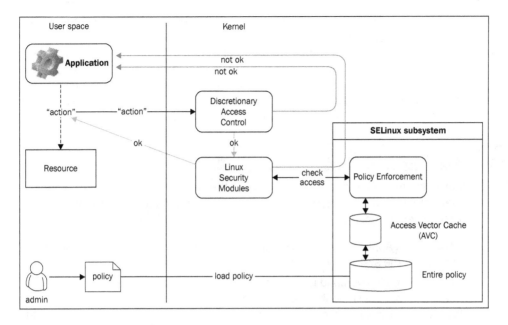

SELinux is a Mandatory Access Control system in which the governed activities on the system are defined in rules that are documented through a policy. This policy is applicable to all processes of the system and enforced through the SELinux subsystem, which is part of the Linux kernel. Anything that is not allowed by the policy will not be allowed at all—security is not left at the discretion of the user or correctness of the application. Unlike Linux DAC restrictions, enforcement itself (the SELinux code) is separate from the rules (the SELinux policy). The rules document what should be considered as acceptable behavior on the system. Actions that do not fit the policy will be denied by the SELinux subsystem.

In SELinux, a set of access control mechanisms are supported. The most visible one is its type enforcement in which privileges of a subject (be it the kernel or a Linux process) towards an object (such as a file, device, system capability, or security control) are granted based on the current security context of that subject. This security context is most often represented through a readable string such as `staff_u:staff_r:staff_t:s0:c0,c3`. This string represents the SELinux user (`staff_u`), SELinux role (`staff_r`), SELinux type/domain (`staff_t`), and optionally, the SELinux sensitivity level or security clearance, which provides both the sensitivity (`s0`) as well as assigned categories (`c0,c3`).

Alongside type enforcement, SELinux has several other features as well. For instance, it provides a **role-based access control** system by assigning valid domains (which are SELinux types assigned to running processes) to roles. If a role is not granted a particular domain, then that role cannot execute tasks or applications associated with that domain. SELinux also supports user-based access controls, thus limiting information flow and governing data sharing between SELinux users.

Another stronghold within SELinux is its support for sensitivities (which SELinux displays as integers, but these integers can very well be interpreted as public, internal, confidential, and so on) as well as access categories. Through the constraints that SELinux can impose in its policy, systems can be made to largely abide by the Bell-LaPadula model (`https://en.wikipedia.org/wiki/Bell-LaPadula_model`). This model supports information flow restrictions such as no read up (lower sensitivities cannot read information from higher sensitivities) and no write down (higher sensitivities cannot leak information to lower sensitivities).

The role of the SELinux policy

The SELinux policy itself is a representation of what the security administrator (the role that is usually mentioned as being the owner of what is and isn't allowed on a system) finds acceptable, expected, and normalized behavior:

- **Acceptable**: Application and user behavior will be acceptable because it will be allowed on the system by the policy
- **Expected**: Application and user behavior will be expected as the policy usually doesn't (or shouldn't) contain access vectors (a permission assigned to a subject towards a particular object) that are not applicable to the system, even if it would be acceptable on other systems in the environment
- **Normalized**: Application and user behavior will be normalized not in the sense of database normalization, but as in normality—something that is consistent with the most common behavior of the process

As a policy represents these behaviors, correct tuning and development of the policy is extremely important. This is why the *SELinux Cookbook* will focus on policy development and policy principles.

A policy that is too restrictive will cause applications to malfunction, often in ways that its users will find unexpected. It will not be surprising to the security administrator of course, as he knows that the policy dictates what is allowed, and he is (or at least should be) perfectly aware of what the policy says.

However, a policy that is too broad will not result in such behavior. On the contrary, everything will work as expected. Sadly, when nonstandard or abnormal behavior is triggered, the (too) broadly defined policy might still allow this nonstandard or abnormal behavior to happen. When this abnormal behavior is an exploited vulnerability, then SELinux—as powerful as it can be—has nothing to deter the exploit, as the policy itself has granted the access. Another example of this principle would be a network firewall, whose policy can be too open as well.

Through the packaged approach that policies provide (SELinux policies are like loadable kernel modules, but then for the SELinux subsystem), administrators can push the policies to one or more systems, usually through the package management system or centralized configuration management system of choice. Unlike Linux DAC controls, which need to be applied on the files themselves, SELinux policies are much easier to handle and are even versionable—a trait much appreciated by administrators in larger environments.

The example

Throughout this book, we will often come across settings that are optional or whose value is heavily dependent on the choices made by the system administrator. In order to not repeat documenting and explaining when a setting or value is configurable, we will use the following configuration settings:

 ▶ The SELinux type (which is configured in `/etc/selinux/config`) will be MCS in this book. It uses an MLS-enabled, single-sensitivity policy definition. This means that contexts will always have a sensitivity level or security clearance assigned when displayed, and the location of the SELinux policy configuration will always be shown in `/etc/selinux/mcs/`. Make sure to substitute this path with your own if the policy store on your environment is named differently. For instance, a Red Hat or Fedora installation defaults to `/etc/selinux/targeted/`.

 ▶ Operations will be documented as they run through restricted users, which are aptly named `user` (for an unprivileged end user assigned the `user_r` role), `staff` (for a user that might perform administrative tasks and is assigned the `staff_r` and `sysadm_r` roles), and `root` (which is mapped to the `sysadm_r` role). Distributions might have users associated with the `unconfined_r` role. Whenever a step can be skipped for unconfined users, it will be explicitly mentioned.

Creating the development environment

We will now create a development environment in which the SELinux policies and upstream project code as well as the functions we use to easily query the SELinux policies will be stored. This environment will have the following three top-level locations:

 ▶ `local/`: This location contains the SELinux rules that are local to the system and not part of a cooperatively developed repository (that is, where other developers work)

 ▶ `centralized/`: This location contains checkouts of the various repositories used in the development environment

 ▶ `bin/`: This location contains the supporting script(s) we will use to query the policy sources as well as troubleshoot the SELinux issues

In this exercise, we will also populate the `centralized/` location with a checkout: the SELinux policy tree that is used by the current system.

Getting ready

Look for a good location where the development environment should be stored. This usually is a location in the user's home directory, such as `/home/staff/dev/selinux/`. Whenever this book references a location with respect to the development environment, it will use the `${DEVROOT}` variable to refer to this location.

Another piece of information that we need is the location of the repository that hosts the SELinux policies of the current system. This location is distribution specific, so consult the distribution site for more information. At the time of writing this book, the policies for Gentoo Linux and Fedora can be found at the following locations:

- ► `https://github.com/sjvermeu/hardened-refpolicy`
- ► `https://git.fedorahosted.org/git/selinux-policy.git`

Whenever version control is used, we will use `git` in this book. Other version control systems exist as well, but this too is outside the scope of this book.

How to do it...

To create the development environment used in this book, perform the following steps:

1. Create the necessary directories:

   ```
   ~$ cd ${DEVROOT}
   ~$ mkdir local centralized bin
   ```

2. Create a checkout of the distributions' SELinux policy tree (which, in this example, is based on the Gentoo Linux repository):

   ```
   ~$ cd ${DEVROOT}/centralized
   ~$ git clone git://git.overlays.gentoo.org/proj/hardened-refpolicy.git
   ```

3. Create a `git` repository for the policies that we will develop throughout this book:

   ```
   ~$ cd ${DEVROOT}/local
   ~$ git init
   ```

4. Add the `functions.sh` script, which is available through the download pack of this book, to the `${DEVROOT}/bin/` location.

5. Edit the `.profile`, `.bashrc`, or other shell configuration files that are sourced when our Linux user logs on to the system, and add in the following code:

   ```
   # Substitute /home/staff/dev/selinux with your DEVROOT
   DEVROOT=/home/staff/dev/selinux
   # Substitute the next location with your distributions' policy
   checkout
   POLICY_LOCATION=${DEVROOT}/centralized/hardened-refpolicy/
   source ${DEVROOT}/bin/functions.sh
   ```

6. Log out and log in again, and verify that the environment is working by requesting the definition of the `files_read_etc_files` interface:

```
~$ seshowif files_read_etc_files
interface(`files_read_etc_files',`
  gen_require(`
    type etc_t;
  ')

  allow $1 etc_t:dir list_dir_perms;
  read_files_pattern($1, etc_t, etc_t)
  read_lnk_files_pattern($1, etc_t, etc_t)
')
```

How it works...

The setup of the development environment helps us deal with policy development for further recipes. The checkout of the distributions' SELinux policy tree is to query the existing policy rules while developing new policies. SELinux does not require to have the policy sources available on a system (only the compiled binary SELinux policy modules and parts of the SELinux policy rules, which can be used by other policy modules). As a result, default installations usually do not have the policy rules available on the system.

By having the checkout at our disposal, we can review the existing SELinux policy files and happily use examples from it for our own use. A major user of this checkout is the `functions. sh` script, which uses the `${POLICY_LOCATION}` variable to know where the checkout is hosted. This script provides several functions that we'll use throughout this book; they will also help in querying the sources.

By sourcing this `functions.sh` script during log on, these functions are readily available in the user's shell. One of these functions is the `seshowif` function, which displays the rules of a particular interface. The example given shows the definition of the `files_read_etc_files` interface, which we used to validate that our setup is working correctly.

The `functions.sh` script can also work with the interface files that are available through `/usr/share/selinux/devel/` (on Fedora/Red Hat systems), making the checkout of the policy repository optional if the user does not need access to the complete policy rules. The policy location defined then is as follows:

```
export POLICY_LOCATION=/usr/share/selinux/devel/
```

There's more...

Next to the distributions' SELinux policy tree, one can also use the reference policy SELinux tree. This is the upstream project that most, if not all, Linux distributions use as the source of their policies. It has to be said though that the reference policy often lags behind on the policy repositories of the individual distributions, as it has stricter acceptance criteria for policy enhancements.

It also doesn't hurt to check out the SELinux policy repositories of other distributions. Often, Linux distributions first do SELinux policy updates on their own repository before pushing their changes to the reference policy (which is called upstreaming in the free software development community). By looking at other distributions' repositories, developers can easily see if the necessary changes have been made in the past already (and are thus more likely to be correct).

See also

For more information about the topics covered in this recipe, refer to the following resources:

- ▶ The reference policy project (`http://oss.tresys.com/projects/refpolicy/`)
- ▶ The Git tutorial (`http://git-scm.com/docs/gittutorial`)

Building a simple SELinux module

Now that we have a development environment, it is time to create our first SELinux policy module. As its purpose does not matter at this point, we will focus on a privilege that is by default not allowed (and rightfully so) yet easy to verify, as we want to make sure that our policy development approach works. The privilege we are going to grant is to allow the system logger to write to a logfile labeled `named_conf_t` (the type used for the configuration of the BIND DNS server—known as `named`).

Building SELinux policy modules is to extend the existing policy with more rules that allow certain accesses. It is not possible to create a policy module that reduces the allowed privileges for a domain. If this is needed, the policy module needs to recreate and substitute the existing policy (and thus, a distribution-provided policy will need to be removed from the system).

Getting ready

Before we get started, we first need to make sure that we can test the outcome of the change. A simple method would be to change the context of the `/var/log/messages` file (or another general logfile that the system logger is configured to use) and send messages through the system logger using the `logger` command:

```
~$ logger "Just a simple log event"
~$ tail /var/log/messages
```

Verify that the message has indeed been delivered by looking at the last lines shown through the `tail` command. Then, change the context and try again. The event should not be shown, and a denial should be logged by the audit daemon:

```
~# chcon -t named_conf_t /var/log/messages
~$ logger "Another simple log event"
~$ tail /var/log/messages
~# ausearch -m avc -ts recent
```

With this in place, we can now create our first simple SELinux module.

How to do it...

Building a new SELinux policy is a matter of going through the following steps:

1. Create a file called `mylogging.te` inside `${DEVROOT}/local` with the following content:

   ```
   policy_module(mylogging, 0.1)
   gen_require(`
     type syslogd_t;
     type named_conf_t;
   ')
   # Allow writing to named_conf_t files
   allow syslogd_t named_conf_t:file { getattr append lock ioctl
   open write };
   ```

2. Copy or link the `Makefile` file available in `/usr/share/selinux/devel/` or `/usr/share/selinux/mcs/include/` (the exact location is distribution specific) to the current directory:

   ```
   ~$ ln -s /usr/share/selinux/devel/Makefile
   ```

3. Build the SELinux policy module through this `Makefile`. The target is to name the (target) policy module with the `.pp` suffix:

   ```
   ~$ make mylogging.pp
   ```

4. Switch to the root user, and if we are logged on through an unprivileged SELinux domain/role, switch to the `sysadm_r` or `secadm_r` role (this is not needed if the current user domain is already `sysadm_t` or `unconfined_t`):

   ```
   ~$ sudo -r sysadm_r -t sysadm_t -s
   ```

5. Now, load the SELinux policy module (which will immediately activate the newly defined SELinux policy):

   ```
   ~# semodule -i mylogging.pp
   ```

6. Verify that the newly defined SELinux policy is active by generating a new log event and by looking at the logfile to see if it has indeed been registered.

7. Commit the newly created files to the repository:

   ```
   ~$ cd ${DEVROOT}/local
   ~$ git add mylogging.te Makefile
   ~$ git commit -m 'Adding mylogging.te which allows the system
   logger to write to the named configuration file type named_conf_t'
   ```

   When verified, reset the context of the logfile using `restorecon /var/log/messages` and remove the policy module from the subsystem using `semodule -r mylogging`. After all, we do not want this rule to stay active.

How it works...

There are three important, new aspects of SELinux policy development that we got in touch with in this recipe:

- A policy source file called `mylogging.te` was created
- A generated, binary policy module called `mylogging.pp` was built
- The binary policy file, `mylogging.pp`, is added to the active policy store on the system

At the end, we committed the file to our local repository. Using version control on policy files is recommended in order to track changes across time. A good hint would be to tag new releases of the policies—if users ever report issues with the policy, you can then ask them for the SELinux policy module version (through `semodule -l`) and use the tags in the repository to easily find rules for that particular policy module.

In the remainder of this book, we will no longer use `git add/commit` so that we can focus on the SELinux recipes.

The policy source file

In the recipe, we created a policy source file called `mylogging.te`, which contains the raw SELinux policy rules. The name, `mylogging`, is not chosen at random; it is a common best practice to name custom modules starting with `my` and followed by the name of the SELinux policy module whose content we are enhancing (in our case, the logging module that provides the SELinux policy for everything that is system-logging related). The `.te` suffix is not just a convention (referring to the type enforcement part of SELinux); the build system requires the `.te` suffix.

The policy module rules start with the `policy_module(...)` call, which tells the build system that the file will become a loadable SELinux policy module with the given name and version. This name and version will be displayed by the `semodule` command if we ask it to list all the currently loaded SELinux policy modules:

```
~# semodule -l
aide   1.8.0
alsa   1.13.0
...
mylogging   0.1
...
```

The best practice is to keep all rules for a single domain within a policy module. If rules for multiple unrelated domains are needed, it is recommended that you create multiple modules, as this isolates the policy rules and makes modifications more manageable.

In this simple example, we did not follow this best practice (yet). Instead, we told the SELinux subsystem that the policy is going to be enhanced with an access vector for `syslogd_t`. The access vector here is to allow this domain a set of permissions against files that are labeled as `named_conf_t`.

The binary policy module

When we called the `Makefile` file, the underlying scripts built a loadable binary SELinux policy module. Such files have the `.pp` suffix and are ready to be loaded into the policy store. The `Makefile` file called might not be installed by default; some distributions require specific development packages to be installed (such as `selinux-policy-devel` in Fedora).

There is no nice way of retrieving the sources of a policy if we are only given the `.pp` file. Sure, there are commands such as `semodule_unpackage` and `sedismod` available, but these will only give a low-level view of the rules, not the original `.te` code. So, make sure to have backups, and as we saw in the example, use a versioning system to control changes across time.

Loading a policy into the policy store

To load the newly created policy into the policy store, we called the `semodule` command. This application is responsible for managing the policy store (which is the set of all SELinux policy modules together with the base policy module) and linking or unlinking the modules together into a final policy.

This final policy (which can be found at `/etc/selinux/mcs/policy`) is then loaded into the SELinux subsystem itself and enforced.

There's more...

Throughout this book, the build system used is based on the reference policy build system. This is a collection of M4 macros and affiliated scripts that make the development of SELinux policies easier. This is, however, not the only way of creating SELinux policies.

When visiting online resources, you might come across SELinux policy modules whose structure looks like the following:

```
module somename 1.0;
require {
  type some_type_t;
  type another_type_t;
}
allow some_type_t another_type_t:dir { read search };
```

Downloading the example code

You can download the example code files for all Packt books you have purchased from your account at `http://www.packtpub.com`. If you purchased this book elsewhere, you can visit `http://www.packtpub.com/support` and register to have the files e-mailed directly to you.

These are policy files that do not use the reference policy build system. To build such files, we first create an intermediate module file with `checkmodule`, after which we package the module file towards a loadable binary SELinux policy with `semodule_package`:

```
~$ checkmodule -M -m -o somename.mod somename.te
~$ semodule_package -m somename.mod -o somename.pp
```

To keep things simple, we will stick to the reference policy build system.

See also

Many topics and areas have been touched upon in this recipe. More information can be found at the following resources:

- ▶ Most Linux distributions have distribution-specific information on how SELinux is integrated in the distribution. For Red Hat, these resources can be reached through `https://access.redhat.com`. For Fedora, use `https://docs.fedoraproject.org`. Gentoo has its documentation at `https://wiki.gentoo.org`.

- ▶ For more information on how to administer SELinux on a system, consult the documentation provided by the distribution or read the *SELinux System Administration* book published by Packt Publishing at `http://www.packtpub.com/selinux-system-administration/book`.

- ▶ Extensive coverage of the SELinux language itself is provided by the SELinux Notebook, which is available online at `http://www.freetechbooks.com/the-selinux-notebook-the-foundations-t785.html`.

Calling refpolicy interfaces

Writing up SELinux policies entirely using the standard language constructs offered by SELinux is doable, but it is prone to error and not manageable in the long term. To support a more simple language construct, the reference policy project uses a set of M4 macros that are expanded with the underlying SELinux policy statements when the policy is built.

The API that policy developers can use can be consulted online, but most systems also have this information available onsite at `/usr/share/doc/selinux-*/`. Finding proper interfaces requires some practice though, which is why one of the functions that we installed earlier (as part of the development environment) simplifies this for us.

In this recipe, we are going to edit the `mylogging.te` file we generated earlier with the right reference policy macro.

How to do it...

To use reference policy interfaces in an SELinux policy module, the following approach can be taken:

1. Use the `sefinddef` function to find permission groups or patterns to write to files:

   ```
   ~$ sefinddef 'file.*write'
   define(`write_files_pattern',`
     allow $1 $3:file write_file_perms;
   ...
   define(`write_file_perms',`{ getattr write append lock ioctl open }')
   ...
   ```

2. Use the `seshowdef` function to show the full nature of the `write_files_pattern` definition:

```
~$ seshowdef write_files_pattern
define(`write_files_pattern',`
  allow $1 $2:dir search_dir_perms;
  allow $1 $3:file write_file_perms;
')
```

3. Use the `sefindif` function to find the interface that will allow writing to `named_conf_t`:

```
~$ sefindif 'write_files_pattern.*named_conf_t'
contrib/bind.if: interface(`bind_write_config',`
contrib/bind.if:   write_files_pattern($1, named_conf_t,
named_conf_t)
```

4. Now, update the `mylogging.te` file to use this function. The file should now look like the following:

```
policy_module(mylogging, 0.2)
gen_require(`
  type syslogd_t;
')
bind_write_config(syslogd_t)
```

 Note the use of the backtick (`` ` ``) and single quote (`'`). Whenever definitions are used, they need to start with a backtick and end with a single quote.

5. Rebuild and reload the policy module, and then rerun the tests we did earlier to verify that this still allows us to write to the `named_conf_t labeled` file.

How it works...

One of the principles behind the build system of the reference policy is that an SELinux policy module should not directly mention SELinux types that are not related to that module. Whenever a policy module needs to define rules against a type that is defined by a different module, interfaces defined by that different module should be used instead.

In our example, we need the interface used by the BIND SELinux policy (which handles the BIND-named daemon policy rules); this interface allows us to write to the BIND DNS server configuration file type (`named_conf_t`). We can check the online API, the API documentation in `/usr/share/doc/selinux-*`, or just guess the interface name. However, in order to be certain that the interface does what we need, we need to query the interface definitions themselves.

That is where the `sefinddef`, `seshowdef`, `sefindif`, and `seshowif` functions come into play. These functions are not part of any SELinux user space—they are provided through the `functions.sh` file we installed earlier and are simple `awk/grep/sed` combinations against the SELinux policy files.

With `sefinddef` (the SELinux find definition), we can search through the support macros (not related to a particular SELinux policy module) for any definition that matches the expression given to it. In this recipe, we gave `file.*write` as the expression to look for. The `seshowdef` (SELinux show definition) function shows us the entire definition of the given pattern.

The `sefindif` (SELinux find interface) function then allows us to find an interface that the SELinux policy provides. In this recipe, we used it to search for the interface that allows a domain to write to the BIND DNS server configuration files. There is also a `seshowif` (SELinux show interface) function that shows us the entire interface definition like the following:

```
~$ seshowif bind_write_config
interface(`bind_write_config',`
  gen_require(`
    type named_conf_t;
  ')
  write_files_pattern($1, named_conf_t, named_conf_t)
  allow $1 named_conf_t:file setattr_file_perms;
')
```

This example interface nicely shows how interfaces are handled by the SELinux reference policy build system. Whenever such an interface is called, one or more arguments are given to the interface. In our case, we passed on `syslogd_t` as the first (and only) argument.

The build system then substitutes every `$1` occurrence in the interface with the first argument, effectively expanding the call to the following code:

```
  write_files_pattern(syslogd_t, named_conf_t, named_conf_t)
  allow syslogd_t named_conf_t:file setattr_file_perms;
```

The call to `write_files_pattern` is then expanded with the definition we saw earlier.

For the policy developer, this is all handled transparently. The sources of the SELinux policy file stay well-formatted and only call the interfaces. It is at build time that the expansion of the various interfaces is done. This allows developers to have nicely segregated, compartmentalized policy definitions.

See also

> ▸ The reference policy project can be found online at `http://oss.tresys.com/projects/refpolicy/`

Creating our own interface

Being able to call interfaces is nice, but when we develop SELinux policies, we will run into situations where we need to create our own interface for the SELinux module we are developing. This is done through a file with an `.if` extension.

In this recipe, we are going to extend the `mylogging` policy with an interface that allows other domains to execute the system log daemon binary (but without running this binary with the privileges of the system logger itself; this would be called a domain transition in SELinux).

How to do it...

1. If our current context is an unprivileged user domain (as unconfined domains are highly privileged and can do almost everything), we can try executing the system logger daemon (`syslog-ng` or `rsyslog`) directly and have it fail as follows:

   ```
   ~$ /usr/sbin/syslog-ng --help
   bash: /usr/sbin/syslog-ng: Permission denied
   ```

2. Now, create the `mylogging.if` file (in the same location where `mylogging.te` is) with the following content, granting all permissions needed to execute the binary:

   ```
   ## <summary>Local adaptation to the system logging SELinux
   policy</summary>

   #########################################
   ## <summary>
   ##      Execute the system logging daemon in the caller domain
   ## </summary>
   ## <desc>
   ##    <p>
   ##      This does not include a transition.
   ##    </p>
   ## </desc>
   ## <param name="domain">
   ##      <summary>
   ##        Domain allowed access.
   ##      </summary>
   ## </param>
   #
   interface(`logging_exec_syslog',`
     gen_require(`
       type syslogd_exec_t;
     ')
     can_exec($1, syslogd_exec_t)
   ')
   ```

3. Create a new SELinux policy module for the user domain; this policy should be able to execute the system logger directly. For instance, for the `sysadm_t` domain, we would create a `mysysadm.te` file with the following content:

```
policy_module(mysysadm, 0.1)
gen_require(`
  type sysadm_t;
')
logging_exec_syslog(sysadm_t)
```

4. Build the `mysysadm` policy module and load it. Then, test to see if the daemon binary can now be executed directly:

```
~$ /usr/sbin/syslog-ng --help
```

How it works...

Let's first look at how the build system knows where the interface definitions are. Then, we'll cover the in-line comment system used in the example.

The location of the interface definitions

Whenever an SELinux policy module is built, the build system sources all interface files it finds at the following locations:

▸ `/usr/share/selinux/mcs/include/*` or `/usr/share/selinux/devel/include/*` (depending on the Linux distribution)

▸ The current working directory

The first location is where the interface files of all the SELinux modules provided by the Linux distribution are stored. The files are inside subdirectories named after particular categories (the reference policy calls these layers, but this is only used to make some structure amongst the definitions, nothing else) such as `contrib/`, `system/`, and `roles/`.

For local development of SELinux policies, this location is usually not writable. If we develop our own policy modules, then this would mean that none of the locally managed SELinux policy files can use interfaces of the other local interface files. The `Makefile` file, therefore, also sources all interface files it finds in the current working directory.

The in-line documentation

Inside the interface file created, we notice a few XML-like structures as comments. These comments are prefixed by a double hash sign (##) and are used by the reference policy build system to generate the API documentation (which can be found at `/usr/share/doc/selinux-*`).

For local policies, this in-line documentation is not used and, thus, not mandatory. However, writing the documentation even for local policies helps us in documenting the rules better. Also, if we ever want to push our changes upstream, this in-line documentation will be requested anyway.

The comment system uses the following constructs:

- Right before an interface definition, we encounter a `<summary>` element, which provides a one-sentence description of the interface

- Additional information can then be provided through a `<desc>` element under which the HTML code can be placed for documenting the interface further

- Every parameter to an interface is documented through a `<param>` entity, which again contains a `<summary>` line

See also

- The reference policy API documentation can be found online at `http://oss.tresys.com/docs/refpolicy/api/`

Using the refpolicy naming convention

The interface names used to simplify policy development can be freely chosen. However, the reference policy itself uses a naming convention to try and structure the names used so that the SELinux policy developers can easily find the interfaces they need—if they exist—and give an unambiguous name to an interface they want to create.

The naming convention for the reference policy is available online at `http://oss.tresys.com/projects/refpolicy/wiki/InterfaceNaming`.

Getting ready

In this recipe, we'll do a pen-and-paper exercise to see how the naming convention works. In the example, we will create interface names for three situations:

- To read all logfiles
- To connect to the HTTP port over TCP
- To not audit getting the attributes of user home directories

How to do it...

1. First we need to figure out the file types that are involved in the situations:

    ❑   Generic logfiles are `var_log_t` (as can be seen by querying the label of `/var/log/`itself):

    ```
    ~$ ls -dZ /var/log
    drwxr-xr-x. root root system_u:object_r:var_log_t:s0 /
    var/log
    ```

    ❑   When we deal with all logfiles, we can safely assume this is handled by an SELinux attribute. Let's look at the attributes for the generic `var_log_t` type:

    ```
    ~$ seinfo -tvar_log_t -x
      var_log_t
        file_type
        non_security_file_type
        mountpoint
        non_auth_file_type
        logfile
    ```

    ❑   The `logfile` attribute looks like an interesting hit. We can now grep through the policy sources to figure out which SELinux policy modules handle the `logfile` attribute, or use `sefindif` (assuming that there are interfaces defined that handle this attribute):

    ```
    ~$ sefindif 'attribute logfile'
    system/logging.if: interface(`logging_log_file',`
    ...
    ```

    ❑   For the logfiles example, the module we need is called `logging` as can be seen from the `sefindif` output. Similarly, we will find that for the HTTP port, the module is `corenet`, and home directories are `userdom`.

2. Next, we check whether there is a modifier. The first two situations have no specific modifier (all the actions are regular verbs). The last example has one: do not audit. In the SELinux policy language, this is known as a `dontaudit` statement.

3. Now, let's look at the verbs involved. This is mostly based on experience, but the situations show that there is a huge correlation between the verbs and the eventually chosen `refpolicy` name (which usually uses SELinux permission names):

    ❑ In the first situation, this is `read`

    ❑ The second one has `connect over TCP`, which is translated into `tcp_connect`

    ❑ The last situation has `getting the attributes`, so it is translated as `getattr`

4. Finally, let's look at the object that is being referenced:

    ❑ In the first situation, this is `all logfiles`, which we will name `all_logs`

    ❑ In the second situation, this is `HTTP port`, so we will name `http_port`

    ❑ The third situation has `user home directories`, so we will name `user_home_dirs`

5. Combining this gives us the following interface names:

    ❑ **Read all logfiles**: `logging_read_all_logs`

    ❑ **Connect to the HTTP port over TCP**: `corenet_tcp_connect_http_port`

    ❑ **Do not audit getting the attributes of user home directories**: `userdom_dontaudit_getattr_user_home_dirs`

How it works...

The naming convention that the reference policy uses is not mandated in a technical manner. Just like with coding styles, naming conventions are made so that collaboration is easier (everyone uses the same naming convention) and searching through the large set of interfaces can be directed more efficiently.

Using the proper naming convention is a matter of exercise. If uncertain, ask around in `#selinux` on `irc://irc.freenode.net` or on the reference policy mailing list.

There's more...

Take some time to look through the interface files available at `/usr/share/selinux/devel/include/`. Next, for the more standard permission-based interface names, there are also interface names used for templates and type assignation.

For instance, there is a template called `apache_content_template`. Through it, additional SELinux types and permissions (used for web applications) are created in one go. Similarly, there is an interface called `apache_cgi_domain` that marks a particular type as being a domain that can be invoked through a web servers' CGI support.

Besides the naming convention, the reference policy also has a style guide available at `http://oss.tresys.com/projects/refpolicy/wiki/StyleGuide`. Like the naming convention, this is purely a human aspect for improved collaboration—there is no consequence of violating the coding style beyond the changes that might not be accepted in the upstream repositories.

Distributing SELinux policy modules

We finish this chapter by explaining how SELinux policy modules can be distributed across multiple systems.

How to do it...

To distribute SELinux policies, complete the following steps:

1. Take into account the different system configurations to which the SELinux policies need to be distributed:

   - If multiple systems have different SELinux policy releases to be active, then build the SELinux policy module against each of these implementations. This is heavily distribution specific. For instance, on Gentoo, this is the version of the `sec-policy/selinux-base` package. On Red Hat and derived distributions, this is the version of the `selinux-policy` package.

   - If multiple SELinux policy types are active (such as `mcs`, `targeted`, and `strict`) and there are both MLS-enabled as well as MLS-disabled policies, then the SELinux policy module will need to be built against both an MLS-enabled policy as well as an MLS-disabled policy. The output of `sestatus` will tell us whether MLS is enabled on an active policy or not:

     ```
     ~$ sestatus | grep MLS
     Policy MLS status:      enabled
     ```

2. Package the resulting `.pp` files and distribute them to the various systems. It is a common best practice to place the `.pp` files inside `/usr/share/selinux/mcs/` (this is for an SELinux policy store named `mcs`, you can adjust it where needed).

3. On each system, make sure that the `.pp` file is loaded through `semodule -I policyfile.pp`.

How it works...

SELinux policy modules (the files ending with `.pp`) contain everything SELinux needs to activate the policy. By distributing these files across many systems (and loading it through the `semodule` command), these systems receive the wanted updates against their current SELinux policy.

Once loaded (and this only needs to happen once, as a loaded module is retained even after the system reboots), one does not really need the `.pp` files anymore (loaded modules are copied inside `/etc/selinux`). However, it is recommended that you keep the policies there so that administrators can reload policies as needed; this might help in troubleshooting the SELinux policy and system permission issues.

There are a few caveats to take into account though:

- ▶ Changes in interfaces
- ▶ Kernel version changes
- ▶ MLS-enabled or MLS-disabled policies

Changes in interfaces

The `.pp` files contain all rules that SELinux needs to enforce the additional policy rules. This includes the (expanded) rules that were part of the interface definition files (the `.if` files) of the module itself as well as the interfaces referred to by the policy module.

When an update against an interface occurs, then all SELinux policy modules that might be affected by the change need to be rebuilt. As there is no simple way to know if a module needs to be rebuilt or not, it is recommended that you rebuild all policy modules every time a change has occurred to at least one interface.

Distributions will handle the rebuilding of the policies and the distribution of the rebuilt policies themselves, but for custom policy modules, we need to do this ourselves.

Kernel version changes

New kernel releases might include updates against the SELinux subsystem. When these updates provide additional features, the binary representation of a policy might be updated. This is then reflected in the binary version of the policy that the kernel supports.

Binary versions are backward compatible, so a system that supports a maximum version of 28 (SELinux's binary versions are integers that are incremented with every change) will also support loading policy modules of a lower binary version:

```
~# sestatus
SELinux status:          enabled
SELinuxfs mount:          /sys/fs/selinux
SELinux root directory:     /etc/selinux
Loaded policy name:      mcs
Current mode:          enforcing
Mode from config file:     enforcing
Policy MLS status:          enabled
Policy deny_unknown status:   denied
Max kernel policy version:   28
```

> When the binary version of an SELinux policy module is higher than the maximum kernel policy version, this SELinux policy module will not load on the target system. A higher version means that the policy uses features that are only available in kernels that support this version, so the administrator will need to update the kernels on those systems to support the higher version or update the SELinux policy module to not use these features so that a rebuild creates a lower-versioned binary SELinux policy module.

MLS or not

SELinux policy modules might contain sensitivity-related information. When a policy module is built, information is added to reflect whether it is built against an MLS-enabled system or not.

Therefore, if we have hosts that have diverse policy usages (some policy stores are MLS-enabled and some are MLS-disabled), then the SELinux policy module will need to be built against both and distributed separately.

Usually, this is done by providing SELinux policy modules for each particular SELinux policy type (be it mcs, strict, or targeted).

2
Dealing with File Labels

In this chapter, we will cover how file labels are set and managed, and learn how to configure the SELinux policy ourselves to use and assign the right file labels. The recipes that this chapter covers are as follows:

- ▶ Defining file contexts through patterns
- ▶ Using substitution definitions
- ▶ Enhancing an SELinux policy with file transitions
- ▶ Setting resource-sensitivity labels
- ▶ Configuring sensitivity categories

Introduction

Setting, resetting, and governing file labels are the most common tasks administrators have to perform on an SELinux-enabled system. The policies that are provided by policy developers as well as Linux distributions offer sane defaults to use, but many implementations harbor different locations for services and files. Companies often install their custom scripts and logfiles in nondefault locations, and many daemons can be configured to support multiple instances on the same system—each of them using a different base directory.

System administrators will know how to set context definitions through the `semanage` application and then reset the contexts of the target files using `setfiles` or `restorecon`:

```
~# semanage fcontext -a -t httpd_sys_content_t "/srv/web/zone/
htdocs(/.*)?"
~# restorecon -RF /srv/web/zone/htdocs
```

This, however, is a local definition, which, if necessary, needs to be exported and imported in order to transfer it to other systems:

```
~# semanage export -f local_selinux.mods
~# semanage import -f local_selinux.mods
```

By moving context definitions into the SELinux policy realm, such definitions can be easily installed on multiple systems and managed centrally as we've seen for SELinux policy modules.

Defining file contexts through patterns

SELinux policy modules can contain file context definitions through their .fc files. In these files, path expressions are used to point to the various locations that should match a particular file context, and class identifiers are used to differentiate file context definitions based on the file class (directories, regular files, symbolic links, and more).

In this recipe, we'll create a mylogging SELinux module, which defines additional path specifications for logging-related contexts. We will use direct file paths as well as regular expressions, and take a look at the various class identifiers.

How to do it...

To define a file context through an SELinux policy module, use the following approach:

1. With matchpathcon, we can check what is the context that the SELinux tools would reset the resource to:

    ```
    ~# matchpathcon /service/log
    /service/log   system_u:object_r:default_t
    ```

2. Create the mylogging.te file in which we mention the types that are going to be used in the definition. It is a best practice to handle types that are not defined by the SELinux module itself through a different SELinux module. In this example though, we also declare var_t to keep the example simple:

    ```
    policy_module(mylogging, 0.2)
    gen_require(`
      type var_t;
      type var_log_t;
      type auditd_log_t;
    ')
    ```

3. Next, create the mylogging.fc file in which we declare the path expressions and their associated file context:

    ```
    /service(/.*)?      gen_context(system_u:object_r:var_t,s0)
    /service/log(/.*)?     gen_context(system_u:object_r:var_log_t,s0)
    ```

```
/service/log/audit(/.*)?    gen_context(system_u:object_r:audit
d_log_t,s0)
/lxc/.*/log  -d  gen_context(system_u:object_r:var_log_t,s0)
/var/opt/oracle/listener\.log  --  gen_
context(system_u:object_r:var_log_t,s0)
```

4. Now, build the policy module and load it:

   `~$ make mylogging.pp`

   `~$ semodule -i mylogging.pp`

5. With `matchpathcon`, we can now verify whether the context known to the SELinux tools is the correct one:

   `~# matchpathcon /service/log`

   `/service/log  system_u:object_r:var_log_t`

How it works...

An SELinux policy module contains everything SELinux needs to properly handle a set of policy rules. This includes the rules themselves (which are declared in a `.te` file) with optional interface declarations (in the `.if` files), which define interfaces that other policies can call in order to generate specific SELinux rules. The third and final part of an SELinux policy module is the related file contexts file —hence the `.fc` file suffix.

 Context declarations in a `.fc` file do not automatically enforce and set these contexts. These are merely definitions used by the SELinux utilities and libraries when a relabeling operation occurs.

This contexts file contains, per line:

- A path expression to which an absolute file path should match
- An optional class identifier to discern contexts (files, directories, sockets, symbolic links, and so on)
- The context to be assigned to this path

Each part of the context definition is whitespace delimited:

`<path>  [<class identifier>]  <context>`

The lines can be ordered to the policy developers' liking. Most developers order paths in an alphabetical order with grouping based on the top-level directory.

Path expressions

The regular expression support in the SELinux tools and libraries is based on **Perl-Compatible Regular Expressions** (**PCRE**).

Of all possible expressions, the simplest expression to use is the one without globbing, such as the following code:

```
/var/opt/oracle/listener\.log
```

An important part of this is the escape of the period—if we don't escape the period, then the PCRE support would treat the period as any character matching not only a `listener.log` file, but also `listener_log` or `listenerslog`.

A very common expression is the one that matches a particular directory and all subdirectories and files inside, which is represented in the following example:

```
/service(/.*)?
```

This ensures that there is always a context definition for a file or directory within.

The order of processing

Given the exhaustive list of path expressions that a regular system has, a file path can match multiple rules, so which one will the SELinux utilities use?

Basically, the SELinux utilities follow the principle of *most specific first*. Given two lines A and B, this is checked in the following order, where the first match wins:

1. If line A has a regular expression in it and B doesn't, then B is more specific.
2. If the number of characters before the first regular expression in line A is less than the number of characters before the first regular expression in line B, then B is more specific.
3. If the number of characters in line A is less than the number of characters in line B, then line B is more specific.
4. If line A does not specify an SELinux type (so that the context part of it is `<<none>>`) and line B does, then line B is more specific.

The SELinux utilities will load in the definitions given through the files available at `/etc/selinux/mcs/contexts/files/`, but will give preference to the ones in `file_contexts.local` (and then `file_contexts.homedirs`) as those are the definitions made by the system administrator locally. However, if a local definition uses a regular expression and a policy-provided definition doesn't, then the policy-provided definition is still used. This is the only exception to the preference rules between the various context files.

The SELinux utilities provide a tool called `findcon` (part of the `setools` or `setools-console` package) that can be used to analyze this ordering, which shows the matching patterns within a single (!) context definition file and orders them from least specific to most specific:

```
~$ findcon /etc/selinux/mcs/contexts/files/file_contexts -p /var/log/aide
/.*     system_u:object_r:default_t:s0
/var/.*     system_u:object_r:var_t:s0
/var/log/.*  system_u:object_r:var_log_t:s0
/var/log/aide(/.*)?  system_u:object_r:aide_log_t:s0
```

If only the actual context definition is needed (and not the full set of matching expressions with the precedence order as `findcon` shows), then `matchpathcon` can be used instead:

```
~# matchpathcon /var/log/aide
/var/log/aide  system_u:object_r:aide_log_t:s0
```

Class identifiers

The second part of the context definition is an optional part—a class identifier. Through a class identifier, developers can tell the SELinux utilities that a context definition is only applicable if the path expression matches a particular file class. If the class identifier is omitted, then any class matches.

If a class identifier is shown, then one (per line) of the following identifiers can be used:

- The '`--`' identifier is used for regular files
- The '`-d`' identifier is used for directories
- The '`-l`' identifier is used for symbolic links
- The '`-b`' identifier is used for block devices
- The '`-c`' identifier is used for character devices
- The '`-p`' identifier is used for FIFO files
- The '`-s`' identifier is used for sockets

Context declaration

The final part of a context definition is the context itself that is to be assigned to all matching resources. It is generated through the `gen_context` macro, as follows:

```
gen_context(system_u:object_r:var_t,s0)
```

The `gen_context` macro is used to differentiate context definitions based on policy features. If the target policy does not support MLS, then only the first argument (`system_u:object_r:var_t`, in the example) is used. If the policy supports MLS but only a single sensitivity (`s0`), then `:s0` is appended to the context. Otherwise, the second argument (coincidentally also `s0` in the example) is appended (with a colon in front).

Generally, contexts only differ on the SELinux type. The SELinux owner and SELinux role of the resource usually remain `system_u` and `object_r` respectively.

A special value for the context is `<<none>>`, like in the following definition:

```
/proc   -d   <<none>>
```

This tells the SELinux utilities that they should never try to set the context of this resource. Whenever an administrator triggers a filesystem relabeling operation, these specific locations will not have their label changed (regardless of their current label). This does *not* mean that an existing context should be removed!

There's more...

In the recipe, we covered how to define labels in great detail. If many changes are made, it makes sense to force a relabel on the entire system. On Red Hat systems, this can be accomplished by creating a flag file and rebooting the system:

```
~# touch /.autorelabel
~# reboot
```

On Gentoo systems, the entire system can be relabeled using the `rlpkg` command:

```
~# rlpkg -a -r
```

On Red Hat systems, the command to relabel the system is called `fixfiles`:

```
~# fixfiles relabel
```

This is also needed if a system has been (temporarily) booted without SELinux support or with SELinux disabled as files will be created that have no file context. When an SELinux-enabled system is booted again, it will mark those files as `unlabeled_t`, which is a type that most domains have no access to (SELinux-wise).

Using substitution definitions

Sometimes, applications and their resources get installed at different locations than expected by the SELinux policy. Trying to accommodate this by defining additional context definitions for each and every subdirectory can easily become unmanageable.

To help administrators, the SELinux utilities support substitution entries, which tell SELinux "if a path starts with *this*, then label it as if it starts with *that*". Administrators can set such a substitution (which is called an **equivalence class**) using `semanage`, as follows:

```
~# semanage fcontext -a -e / /mnt/chroots/bind
```

In this example, any location under `/mnt/chroots/bind/` will be labeled as if it started from the main `/` directory (so `/mnt/chroots/bind/etc/` becomes `etc_t` as `/etc/` is `etc_t`).

Target locations for `chroots` are a good use case for this. A `chroot` is an alternate location on the filesystem, which will act as the root filesystem for one or a set of applications.

For administrators who want to set substitutions across multiple systems, it is not possible to make this part of an SELinux policy module. The file that we need to manage is called `file_contexts.subs` (there is also one that ends with `.subs_dist` and is managed by the Linux distribution, which we will not touch). Having that said, we can always look at how to update this file in a more or less sane manner.

Getting ready

The easiest method would be to use a central configuration management utility, such as Puppet, CFEngine, Chef, or Ansible, as these systems allow administrators to force the content of specific files to a particular value. The use of a configuration management tool is an entire book in itself, so this is outside the scope of this book. If you do want to pursue this, remember that the `file_contexts.subs` file is (also) managed by the `semanage` command. Administrators might want to add in local definitions that the central configuration management utility isn't aware of (and thus might revert the change).

In this recipe, we'll cover a generic approach, but it does require that there is a way to do both a file transfer followed by a single line command (executed with proper permissions). This, however, shouldn't be much of a challenge to most system administrators.

How to do it...

In order to apply changes to a wide range of systems, follow the next set of steps:

1. Apply the change locally to the system:

   ```
   ~# semanage fcontext -a -e / /mnt/chroot/bind
   ```

2. Export the definitions to a single file:

   ```
   ~# semanage export -f local_selinux.mods
   ```

3. Edit the `local_selinux.mods` file and remove all entries that are not related to the change but need to be distributed.

4. Distribute the resulting file to the target systems.

5. Apply the changes locally to the system:

```
~# semanage import -f local_selinux.mods
```

How it works...

The `semanage fcontext` command instantiates an equivalence class for `/mnt/chroot/bind/`, which has all subdirectories and files inside of it labeled as if they were at `/`. This ensures that administrators do not need to define a large amount of file contexts for each and every `chroot` location they manage.

However, this might become problematic as `semanage fcontext` only applies changes locally, and on a larger infrastructure, the same settings might need to be applied to multiple systems. For this, `semanage export` and `semanage import` can be used.

The output of the `semanage export` command is a set of instructions for `semanage` and follows the syntax of the `semanage` commands to the letter.

When exporting the `semanage` definitions, the first set of commands that are stored are the `delete all` statements such as `fcontext -D` (delete all locally made `semanage fcontext` settings). Of course, if we only need to distribute the substitution definitions, then deleting all previously made local statements is incorrect. Hence, the need to manually edit the `local_selinux.mods` file. If only the equivalence class definition needs to be distributed, then the file might just contain the following:

```
fcontext -a -e / /mnt/chroot/bind
```

The exported file can then be distributed to all target systems and loaded through the `semanage import` command effectively applying the same set of changes to the system.

If the definition was already applied on a system, then the `import` command will fail:

```
~# semanage import -f local_selinux.mods
ValueError: Equivalence class for /mnt/chroot/bind already exists
```

It is important to note here that if one command in the file fails to apply, then none of the commands in the file are applied (the file is processed in one go). This is why the `delete all` rules are originally made part of the exported set of commands.

This makes distributed management of such settings more challenging if locally applied changes need to be kept as well, unless the distributed set of changes are singular (one exported instruction, which is allowed to fail).

There's more...

Most files inside the `/etc/selinux/mcs/contexts/` location shouldn't be managed through any tool except either the Linux distribution package management system (through the installation of the base SELinux policy) or `semanage`.

That being said, most files inside this location don't change much (except for the `files/file_contexts` file). It might be beneficial to hook into the package management system to update these files (if supported) or bluntly take over the management of these files, assuming you track the changes that the distribution would make closely.

See also

The following resources dive deeper into the topics discussed in this recipe:

- ▸ To find out more about the various configuration files, check out `http://selinuxproject.org/page/PolicyConfigurationFiles`
- ▸ The interaction of SELinux with `chroots` is discussed in more detail in *Chapter 9, Aligning SELinux with DAC*

Enhancing an SELinux policy with file transitions

Up until now, we've only handled the configuration part on file contexts: if we would ask SELinux utilities to relabel files, then the changes we made would come into effect. However, unless you run with the `restorecond` daemon checking out all possible file modifications (which would really be a resource hog) or run `restorecon` manually against all files regularly, the newly defined contexts will not be applied to the files.

What we need to do is modify the local SELinux policy so that, upon creation of these files, the Linux kernel automatically assigns the right label to those files. This is handled through file transitions, which is a specific case of a **type transition**.

In a type transition, we configure a policy so that if a given domain creates a file (or other resource class) inside a directory with a specified label, then the created object should automatically get a specific label. Policy-wise, this is written as follows:

```
type_transition <domain> <directory_label>:<resource_class> <specific_label>
```

SELinux has also added in support for named file transitions (from Linux 2.6.39 onwards, and available in Gentoo, Fedora 16+, and Red Hat Enterprise Linux 7+). In that case, such a transition only occurs if the created resource matches a particular filename exactly (so no regular expressions):

```
type_transition <domain> <directory_label>:<resource_class>
<specific_label> <filename>
```

Through the reference policy macro's, this is supported with the `filetrans_pattern` definition.

Getting ready

In order to properly define file transitions, we need to know what the source domain is that is responsible for creating the resource. For instance, a `/var/run/snort/` directory might be created by an `init` script, but if there is no file transition, then this directory will be created with the type of the parent directory (which is `var_run_t`) instead of the proper type (`snort_var_run_t`).

So make sure to write down all the involved labels (as an example, we will use `initrc_t` for an `init` script, `var_run_t` for the parent directory, and `snort_var_run_t` for the target directory) before embarking on this recipe.

How to do it...

Defining a file transition can be done as follows:

1. Search through the SELinux policies to see if there is an interface that will provide a file transition from a given domain to `snort_run_t`:

   ```
   ~$ sefindif filetrans.*snort_var_run_t
   ```

2. Assuming that none have been found, search for interfaces that allow `initrc_t` created resources to transition to a given type:

   ```
   ~$ sefindif filetrans.*initrc_t
   system/init.if: interface(`init_daemon_pid_file',`
   system/init.if:    files_pid_filetrans(initrc_t, $1, $2, $3)
   ```

3. Bingo! Now, let's create an enhancement for the snort SELinux module (through a `mysnort` policy file) with the following declaration in it:

   ```
   policy_module(mysnort, 0.1)
   gen_require(`
     type snort_t;
     type snort_var_run_t;
   ')
   ```

```
# If initrc_t creates a directory called "snort" in a var_run_t
dir,
# make sure this one is immediately labeled as snort_var_run_t.
init_daemon_pid_file(snort_var_run_t, dir, "snort")
```

4. Build the new policy and load it. Then check with `sesearch` if a type transition is indeed declared:

```
~$ sesearch -s initrc_t -t var_run_t -T | grep "snort"
type_transition initrc_t var_run_t : dir snort_var_run_t "snort"
```

How it works...

Linux distributions that support SELinux already provide an SELinux policy that works in a majority of deployments. The default policy is extensive and works mostly out of the box. If specific changes are needed, chances are that these particular SELinux rules are already defined (as part of policy interfaces) and only need to be instantiated and loaded.

Policy interfaces usually exist in the following two types:

▶ Interfaces whose subject is delivered through an argument, and where the object (against which operations are performed) and perhaps target (in our case, to which a transition should occur) are hardcoded

▶ Interfaces whose subject is hardcoded and where the object, target, or both are arguments to the interface

An example of the first interface type that can be used in our example would look like the following code:

```
interface(`snort_generic_pid_filetrans_pid',`
  gen_require(`
    type snort_var_run_t;
  ')
  files_pid_filetrans($1, snort_var_run_t, dir, $2)
')
```

We could then call this interface like this:

```
snort_generic_pid_filetrans_pid(initrc_t, "snort")
```

However, such interfaces would be a burden to maintain. For every daemon support added to the system, the `init` policy would need to be changed with a named file transition together with the newly added policy rules for the daemon. Considering the amount of daemons that can run on a system, the `init` policy would literally be filled with a massive amount of named file transitions—at least one for every daemon.

The interface declaration that we encountered in the example is much more manageable. The interface is meant to be called by the daemon policy itself and immediately ensures that the `initrc_t` type can create directories of the given type (`snort_var_run_t`) inside the generic run directory (`var_run_t`). New additions to the policy leave the `init` policy at rest, making maintenance of the policies easier.

Finding the right search pattern

To find the right pattern, we use the `sefindif` interface to search through the available interfaces. Finding the right expression is a matter of experience.

As we know, we want to search for file transitions, the line we are looking for will contain `filetrans_pattern`. Then, one of the arguments involved is the type we are going to transition to (`snort_var_run_t`). So the expression we used in the example was changed to `filetrans.*snort_var_run_t`. As that didn't result in anything, the next search involved the domain from which a transition has to be made (`initrc_t`) so that the expression was changed to `filetrans.*initrc_t`.

However, let's assume we don't know that `filetrans_pattern` needs to be searched for. The type itself (`snort_var_run_t`) or domain (`initrc_t`) might be sufficient to search through, like in the following searches:

```
~$ sefindif snort_var_run_t
~$ sefindif initrc_t
```

From the resulting list of interfaces, we can then see if an interface is available that suits our needs.

Patterns

Patterns such as `filetrans_pattern` are important supporting definitions inside the reference policy. They bundle a set of permissions related to a functional approach (such as read files, which are handled through a `read_files_pattern`) and are not tied to a particular type (unlike interfaces).

The need for patterns comes from the very fine-grained access controls that SELinux has on Linux activities. Reading a file is a nice example: it is not sufficient to just allow a type to perform the `read` action:

```
allow initrc_t snort_var_run_t:file read;
```

Most applications first check the attributes of the file (`getattr`) and open the file before they can read the file. Depending on the purpose, they might also want to lock the file or perform I/O operations on it through `ioctl`. So instead of just the preceding access vector, the rule was changed to:

```
allow initrc_t snort_var_run_t:file { getattr lock open read ioctl }
```

The reference policy provides a single permission set for this called `read_file_perms`, which turns the access vector into the following:

```
allow initrc_t snort_var_run_t:file read_file_perms;
```

Second, the policy developers often want to allow a domain to read a file inside a directory that is labeled similarly. For instance, a `snort_var_run_t` file can be at `/var/run/snort/snort.pid` with the `/var/run/snort/` directory also being labeled as `snort_var_run_t`. So we would also need to grant the `initrc_t` type search rights inside the directory—which again is a set of permissions as can be seen from the `search_dir_perms` definition:

```
~$ seshowdef search_dir_perms
define(`search_dir_perms',`{ getattr search open }')
```

Instead of creating multiple rules for this, a pattern is created, called `read_files_pattern`, which looks like the following:

```
~$ seshowdef read_files_pattern
define(`read_files_pattern',`
  allow $1 $2:dir search_dir_perms;
  allow $1 $3:file read_file_perms;
')
```

This allows policy developers to use a single call:

```
read_files_pattern(initrc_t, snort_var_run_t, snort_var_run_t)
```

To see the various patterns supported for policy development, use `sefinddef` with the 'define.*_pattern' expression:

```
~$ sefinddef define.*_pattern
```

Using patterns allows developers to create readable policy rules using a functional approach rather than a full sum-up of each individual access vector.

There's more...

In the `snort_generic_pid_filetrans_pid` interface presented earlier, we used a named file transition: the transition occurs only if the filename passed on as the last argument matches the filename of the file created.

Named file transitions take precedence over normal file transitions. A good example for this are the file transitions supported for the `initrc_t` domain:

```
~# semanage -s initrc_t -t var_run_t -T
Found 2 semantic te rules:
   type_transition initrc_t var_run_t : file initrc_var_run_t;
   type_transition initrc_t var_run_t : dir initrc_var_run_t;
Found 16 named file transition rules:
type_transition initrc_t var_run_t : dir udev_var_run_t "udev";
type_transition initrc_t var_run_t : dir tor_var_run_t "tor";
...
```

In this case, if an `init` script creates a directory called `udev` or `tor` (or any of the other transition rules that are not shown in the example), then a proper file transition occurs. If the filename doesn't match, then a transition occurs to the `initrc_var_run_t` type.

File transitions on regular files and directories are the most common, but transitions can also occur on various other classes, such as sockets, FIFO files, symbolic links, and more.

See also

▸   Domain transitions (which assign a different context to a process rather than a file) are covered in *Chapter 3, Confining Web Applications* in more detail and are used in *Chapter 4, Creating a Desktop Application Policy* and *Chapter 5, Creating a Server Policy*

Setting resource-sensitivity labels

When an SELinux policy is MLS-enabled and supports multiple sensitivities (which is not the case with MCS, as MCS only has a single sensitivity), then SELinux can govern information flow and access between a domain and one or more resources based on the clearance of the domain and the sensitivity level of the resource. But even with a single sensitivity (as is the case with MCS), SELinux has additional constraint support to ensure that domains cannot access resources that have one of the categories assigned that the domain doesn't have clearance for.

A sensitivity level consists of a sensitivity (s0 is generally being used for the lowest sensitivity and s15—which is a policy build-time constant and thus can be configured—is the highest sensitivity) together with a category set (which can be a list such as c0,c5,c8.c10).

A security clearance is similar to a sensitivity level but shows a sensitivity range (such as s0-s3) instead of a single sensitivity level. A security clearance can be seen as a range going from the lowest sensitivity level to the highest sensitivity level allowed by the domain.

When policies are being developed for such systems, context definitions and policy rules can take sensitivities into account. In this recipe, we will do the two most common operations for MLS-enabled systems:

- Define a context with a higher-level sensitivity
- Set the clearance of a process policy-wise on a domain transition

To accomplish this, we will use the snort intrusion detection system as an example, forcing it to be always executed with the s3 sensitivity and all possible categories.

This example will also show us how to substitute an existing policy rather than enhance it, as we are going to update a definition that would otherwise collide with the existing definition.

How to do it...

To modify an existing domain to support specific sensitivity levels, execute the following steps:

1. Copy the snort.te and snort.fc files from the distribution policy repository to the local environment:

   ```
   ~$ cp ${POLICY_LOCATION}/policy/modules/contrib/snort.*
   ${DEVROOT}/local
   ```

2. Rename the files to mysnort (or customsnort), so we always know this is a customized policy. Don't forget to update the policy_module call in the .te file.

3. Open the mysnort.te file and look for the init_daemon_domain call. Substitute the call with the following:

   ```
   init_ranged_daemon_domain(snort_t, snort_exec_t,  s3:mcs_allcats)
   ```

4. In mysnort.fc, label the snort resources with the s3 sensitivity. For instance, for the snort binary, label it as follows:

   ```
   /usr/bin/snort  --  gen_context(system_u:object_r:snort_exec_t,s3)
   ```

5. Build the mysnort policy, remove the currently loaded snort SELinux policy module, and load the mysnort one:

   ```
   ~# /etc/init.d/snort stop
   ~# semodule -r snort
   ~# semodule -i mysnort.pp
   ```

6. Relabel all files related to snort and then start snort again.

How it works...

There are three important aspects to this recipe:

1. We replace the entire policy rather than create an enhancement.
2. We update the policy to use a ranged daemon domain.
3. We update the file contexts to use the right sensitivity.

The file context update is obvious but the reason for fully replacing the policy might not be.

Full policy replacement

In the example, we copied the existing policy for the snort SELinux module and made the updates in the copy, rather than trying to enhance the policy by creating an additional module.

This is needed because we are making changes to the SELinux policy that are mutually exclusive to the already running SELinux policy. For instance, the file context changes would confuse SELinux as it would then have two fully matching definitions through policy modules, but each with a different resulting context.

In the example, we only copied the type enforcement declarations (`snort.te`) and file context declarations (`snort.fc`). If we would copy the interface definitions as well (`snort.if`), the policy build would give us a warning that there are duplicate interface definitions—the ones provided by the Linux distribution are still on the system after all.

Ranged daemon domain

In the SELinux policy itself, we substituted the `init_daemon_domain(snort_t, snort_exec_t)` entry with the following:

```
init_ranged_daemon_domain(snort_t, snort_exec_t, s3:mcs_allcats)
```

Let's take a look at the contents of this interface:

```
~$ seshowif init_ranged_daemon_domain
interface(`init_ranged_daemon_domain',`
  gen_require(`
    type initrc_t;
  ')
  init_daemon_domain($1, $2)
  ifdef(`enable_mcs',`
    range_transition initrc_t $2:process $3;
  ')
  ifdef(`enable_mls',`
```

```
   range_transition initrc_t $2:process $3;
   mls_rangetrans_target($1)
  ')
')
```

The newly called interface calls the original init_daemon_domain, but enhances it with MCS- and MLS-related logic. In both cases, it calls range_transition so that when the snort init script (running as initrc_t) transitions to the snort_t domain, then the active sensitivity range is also changed to the third parameter.

In our case, the third parameter is s3:mcs_allcats, where mcs_allcats is a definition that expands to all categories supported by the policy (such as c0.c255 if the policy supports 256 categories).

In case of MLS, it also calls mls_rangetrans_target, which is an interface that sets an attribute to the snort_t domain, which is needed for the MLS constraints enabled in the policy.

From the expanded code, we can see that there are ifdef() statements. These are blocks of SELinux policy rules that are enabled (or ignored) based on build-time parameters. The enable_mcs and enable_mls parameters are set if an MCS or MLS policy is enabled. Other often used build-time parameters are distribution selections (such as distro_redhat if the SELinux policy rules are specific for Red Hat Enterprise Linux and Fedora systems) and enable_ubac (which is when user-based access control is enabled).

Constraints

Most, if not all, SELinux policy development focuses on type enforcement rules and context definitions. SELinux does support various other statements, one of which is the constrain statement used to implement constraints.

A constraint restricts permissions further based on a set of expressions that cover not only the type of the object or subject, but also SELinux role and SELinux user. The constraint that is related to the mlsrangetrans attribute (which is set by the mls_rangetrans_target interface) looks like the following:

```
mlsconstrain process transition
    (( h1 dom h2 ) and
    (( l1 eq l2 ) or ( t1 == mlsprocsetsl ) or
    (( t1 == privrangetrans ) and ( t2 == mlsrangetrans )))));
```

The constraint tells us the following things about a transition:

- The transition can occur only when the highest sensitivity level of the subject (domain/actor) dominates the highest sensitivity level of the object
- The lowest sensitivity level of the subject is the same as the lowest sensitivity level of the object

- If not, then the type of the subject has to have the `mlsprocsetsl` attribute set
- If not, then both of the following statements have to be true:

   - The type of the subject has the `privrangetrans` attribute set
   - The type of the object has the `mlsrangetrans` attribute set

Domination means that the sensitivity level of the first security level is equal to or higher than the sensitivity level of the second security level, and the categories of the first security level are the same or a superset of the categories of the second security level.

Constraints in the SELinux policy are part of the base policy set—this means that we are not able to add constraints through loadable SELinux policies. If we want to include additional constraints, we would need to build the entire policy ourselves, patching the `constraints`, `mls`, and `mcs` files inside the policy repository's `policy/` subdirectory.

Knowing about constraints is important, but we probably never need to write constraints ourselves.

See also

The SELinux project site is a good start for learning about constraints and their related statements:

- The MLS statements at `http://selinuxproject.org/page/NB_MLS`
- The constraint statements at `http://selinuxproject.org/page/ConstraintStatements`

Configuring sensitivity categories

Although MCS policies are MLS-enabled, they are configured to only support a single sensitivity (namely `s0`). Yet even with this limitation, an MCS policy can be very useful, for instance, in situations where a system hosts services for multiple customers. This is because MCS can still benefit from security clearances based on categories.

Unlike sensitivities, categories are more like a discretionary access control system. Categories are meant to be used by users (or administrators) to label files and other resources as being a member of one or more categories. Access to those resources is then based on the clearance level of the process and the categories assigned to the resource. Categories are also not hierarchically structured.

An example of a use case where categories play a major role is in multitenant deployments: systems that host one or more services for multiple tenants (multiple customers), which, of course, require proper security segregation so that one tenant cannot access resources of another tenant.

In most cases, administrators will try to separate those services through the runtime user (and group membership). This is, however, not always possible. There are situations where these separate processes still need to run as the same runtime user (although with support for additional Linux security subsystems—such as capabilities—the number of situations has significantly reduced again).

In this recipe, we'll configure a system to use multiple categories to differentiate between resources of different customers for a web server that the customers also have shell access to. Through categories, we can provide more protection for the resources of other customers, in case one of the customers is able to execute an exploit that would elevate their privileges.

Getting ready

You need to prepare a system for the multiple tenants. For instance, we can host the entire website content in `/srv/web/<companyname>/` and have the web server configuration at `/etc/apache/conf/<companyname>/`.

In this recipe, as an example, we will configure the system for two companies called `CompanyX` and `CompanyY`. Each company also has a regular user (`userX` for the first company and `userY` for the second).

How to do it...

To instantiate different categories, follow this approach:

1. Settle on the category naming (and numbers) for different customers and configure those in the `setrans.conf` file inside `/etc/selinux/mcs/`:

   ```
   s0:c100=CompanyX
   s0-s0:c100=CompanyXClearance
   s0:c101=CompanyY
   s0-s0:c101=CompanyYClearance
   ```

2. Restart the `mcstrans` service so that it is aware of this configuration.

3. List the categories to make sure that the changes are properly interpreted:

   ```
   ~$ chcat -L
   s0      SystemLow
   s0-s0:c0.c1023   SystemLow-SystemHigh
   s0:c0.c1023   SystemHigh
   s0:c100      CompanyX
   s0-s0:c100   CompanyXClearance
   s0:c101      CompanyY
   s0-s0:c101   CompanyYClearance
   ```

4. Create SELinux users that have clearance to handle the right categories:

   ```
   ~# semanage user -a -L s0 -r CompanyXClearance -R "user_r" userX_u
   ~# semanage user -a -L s0 -r CompanyYClearance -R "user_r" userY_u
   ```

5. Configure the Linux users (logins) with the right security clearance:

   ```
   ~# semanage login -m -s userX_u userX
   ~# semanage login -m -s userX_u userY
   ```

6. Set the right category on the company resources:

   ```
   ~# chcon -l CompanyX -R /srv/web/www.companyX.com/ /etc/apache/
   conf/companyX/
   ```

   ```
   ~# chcon -l CompanyY -R /srv/web/www.companyY.com/ /etc/apache/
   conf/companyY/
   ```

7. Configure the Apache `init` scripts to launch Apache with the right security level by launching it through `runcon`. For instance, on a Red Hat Enterprise Linux 6 system for the first company's web server, the following script is used:

   ```
   LANG=$HTTPD_LANG daemon --pidfile=${pidfile} runcon -t httpd_t -l
   CompanyX $httpd $OPTIONS
   ```

8. (Re)start the web server and validate that it is running with the right security level:

   ```
   ~# ps -efZ | grep httpd
   ```

How it works...

We started by configuring the system so that we can name categories and ranges rather than having to use the integer representations. Next, we created an SELinux user for each company and assigned each (regular) Linux account to the right SELinux user. After updating the contexts of all company-related files, we configured Apache to start in the right context.

The mcstrans and setrans.conf files

The `setrans.conf` file is a regular text file that the MCS transition daemon (`mcstransd`) uses to substitute the real security level (such as `s0:c100`) with a human readable string (such as `CompanyX`).

The Linux utilities themselves (such as `ls` and `ps`) use the SELinux libraries to get information about the contexts of files and processes. These libraries then connect with the `mcstransd` process (through the `/var/run/setrans/.setrans-unix` socket), sending the real security level and retrieving the human-readable representation for it.

It is important to remember that this is only a representation and not how the security level is stored. In other words, do not use this in file context definition files (that is, the SELinux policy .fc files).

SELinux users and Linux user mappings

In the example, an SELinux user is created for each company. This SELinux user is given the clearance to work with resources tagged with the category of the respective companies. The real Linux accounts are then mapped to this SELinux user.

From the example, we see that there are two definitions for each company:

```
s0:c100      CompanyX
s0-s0:c100   CompanyXClearance
```

The first one is a security level and can be assigned to both resources as well as processes (users). The second one is a security clearance (a range). In this particular example, the clearance tells us that the high security level (which can be seen as *what the process is allowed to access*) are the resources of the company (s0:c100), and the low security level (which can be seen as *the security level of the process itself*) is just s0.

The users for the company, therefore, have clearance to access the files (and other resources) that have their company's category assigned to it. However, all activities performed by these user accounts do not get this category by default—the users will need to use chcon to set the category, as follows:

```
~$ chcon -l CompanyX public_html/index.html
```

It is possible to give the users the security level itself rather than the clearance. When that occurs, any resource created by the user will also get the proper category set. But, do not use this as a way to confine resources—users can always remove categories from resources.

Granting the security level can be done on the SELinux user level, but it is also possible to do this through the SELinux user mapping as long as the range passed on is dominated by the range set on the SELinux user level. For instance, to set CompanyX (s0:c100) as the security level rather than CompanyXClearance, which is the default for users mapped to the userX_u SELinux user, the following command can be used:

```
~# semanage login -m -r CompanyX user1
```

Running Apache with the right context

The last change made in the example was to configure the system to start the web server with the right security level. This is done through the runcon command, where we pass on the sensitivity level (and not the security clearance) to make sure that every resource created through the web server inherits the right category as well as the target type.

The SELinux policy knows that if an `init` script launches the Apache binary (`httpd`), then this application has to run in the `httpd_t` domain. However, now the `init` script launches `runcon`—which the SELinux policy sees as a regular binary—so the application would continue to run in the `initrc_t` domain. Hence, we need to pass on the target type (`httpd_t`). On systems with an SELinux policy without unconfined domains, forgetting this would prevent the web server to run. On systems with an SELinux policy with unconfined domains, this might result in the web server to run in an unconfined domain (`initrc_t`), effectively disabling the SELinux protections we need for the web server!

See also

The following are some more examples on multitenancy and how SELinux interacts with it:

- ▶ sVirt (`http://selinuxproject.org/page/SVirt`) uses SELinux categories to segregate virtual guests from one another

- ▶ Linux containers, such as through the LXC project (`https://linuxcontainers.org`), use SELinux for further isolation of containers from the main system

- ▶ Apache has support for multitenancy through the `mod_selinux` module, which is covered in *Chapter 3, Confining Web Applications*

3
Confining Web Applications

In this chapter, we will cover the default confinement of the web server domain and practice how to enhance this policy to suit our needs. We will also look into `mod_selinux` and how it can be used to confine web applications even further. All this will be handled through the following recipes:

- ▶ Listing conditional policy support
- ▶ Enabling user directory support
- ▶ Assigning web content types
- ▶ Using different web server ports
- ▶ Using custom content types
- ▶ Creating a custom CGI domain
- ▶ Setting up mod_selinux
- ▶ Starting Apache with limited clearance
- ▶ Mapping HTTP users to contexts
- ▶ Using source address mapping to decide on contexts
- ▶ Separating virtual hosts with mod_selinux

Introduction

Web applications are a prime example of where SELinux can prove its effectiveness. They are often facing the (untrusted) Internet and are a popular target to exploit. Securing the web server and web applications is just one of the basic mitigating strategies though—by confining the web server, we are reducing the results of a successful exploit even further.

A well-confined web server will only allow operations towards the operating system that are acceptable behavior for the service. But considering the wide area of services that can be provided through a web server, we must be careful not to open up too many privileges.

Policy developers have foreseen the situation that the web server domain might be too broad in its privileges and have made the web server domain (`httpd_t`) not only very versatile, but also very configurable. In this chapter, we will look into the domain in more detail.

Listing conditional policy support

The first configurable aspect of the SELinux web server domain policy is its wide use of SELinux Booleans. Through these Booleans, additional policy rules can be selectively enabled or disabled. In this recipe, we'll look at the Booleans and see how these can be toggled.

How to do it...

In order to list the conditional policy support, execute the following steps:

1. Request the list of all SELinux Booleans and selectively show those starting with `httpd_`:

   ~# **getsebool -a | grep httpd_**

2. To get a short description together with the Booleans, we can use `semanage`:

   ~# **semanage boolean -l | grep httpd_**

3. If the description of a Boolean isn't sufficient, we can ask the SELinux utilities to display the SELinux rules that will be enabled (or disabled) if the Boolean is set:

   ~# **sesearch -b httpd_enable_ftp_server -AC**

   Found 3 semantic av rules:

   DT allow httpd_t httpd_t : capability net_bind_service ;
   [httpd_enable_ftp_server]

   DT allow httpd_t ftp_port_t : tcp_socket { recv_msg send_msg name_bind } ; [httpd_enable_ftp_server]

   DT allow httpd_t ftp_server_packet_t : packet { send recv } ; [httpd_enable_ftp_server]

How it works...

Conditional SELinux policy support is provided through SELinux Booleans. These are configurable parameters (with a `true`/`false` value), which an administrator can enable or disable using the `setsebool` or `semanage boolean` command.

With the `getsebool` command, we request an overview of all SELinux Booleans. Recent policies have a few hundred Booleans assigned, but luckily most Booleans follow one of the two following naming conventions that make filtering easier:

- A Boolean starts with `allow_` or `use_`
- A Boolean starts with the SELinux policy module prefix

Booleans that start with `allow_` or `use_` are considered global Booleans and will usually affect multiple SELinux policy modules. A good example for such a Boolean is `allow_execmem`, which enables several domains to execute code stored in writable memory rather than read-only memory (this is a harmful, but sometimes unavoidable memory permission setting).

Most, if not all other Booleans start with the SELinux policy module prefix that they are applied to. For the web server, this is `httpd_` (even though the policy is called apache, the `httpd_` prefix is chosen because the policy can apply directly on various web servers, not only on the Apache HTTPd).

When we use the `semanage boolean` command, a short description is provided for the Booleans. This description is obtained from an XML file called `policy.xml`, which can be found at `/usr/share/selinux/devel/`. The XML file is generated during the build of the base SELinux policy.

The most accurate description of a Boolean, however, is the set of rules that it would trigger when enabled or disabled. This is where the `sesearch` command comes into play.

As can be seen from the example, Booleans will trigger one or more allow rules. The prefix to the `sesearch` output tells us whether a shown rule is active if the Boolean is true (`T`) or false (`F`), and if the rule is currently enabled (`E`) in the policy or disabled (`D`).

A nice trick when querying the SELinux policy using `sesearch` is to ask for Boolean-managed rules as well (regardless of whether they are currently enabled or disabled). This can be accomplished by adding the `-C` option (which is the short option for `--show_cond`). For instance, to find the transitions of the `newrole_t` domain, the following command can be used:

```
~# sesearch -s newrole_t -c process -p transition -AC
Found 5 semantic av rules:
   allow newrole_t newrole_t : process { … };
   allow newrole_t chkpwd_t : process transition;
   allow newrole_t updpwd_t : process transition;
EF allow newrole_t userdomain : process transition ; [ secure_mode ]
DT allow newrole_t unpriv_userdomain : process transition ; [ secure_mode
]
```

See also

▸ The `httpd_selinux` manual page lists all SELinux Booleans that are applicable to the Apache SELinux module and explains their purpose in more detail:

```
~$ man httpd_selinux
```

Enabling user directory support

Let's look at an example of how to use SELinux Booleans applicable to web server installations. In this recipe, we'll enable Apache UserDir support (allowing the web server to serve local user account web pages at `http://sitename/~username`).

Getting ready

Configure the Apache web server to serve user content. An entire Apache configuration tutorial would be in place here, but this is not in the scope of this book. Basically, this is done by editing the `httpd.conf` file and setting the `UserDir` directive.

How to do it...

To enable user directory support, follow the next set of steps:

1. Make sure that the user's home directory is accessible for the Apache runtime account with the following commands. If Linux DAC denies access, SELinux will not even handle the request.

   ```
   ~$ chmod 755 ${HOME}/
   ~$ chmod 755 ${HOME}/public_html
   ```

2. Check that access isn't already allowed by surfing to a user page. If all permissions are okay but SELinux denies access, then the page should be served with a 403 (forbidden) error and a denial should be registered in the audit logs. The Apache error logs would yield a permission denied against the resource.

3. The audit logs will probably tell that `httpd_t` isn't allowed to act on `home_root_t` or `user_home_dir_t`. From a look through the SELinux Booleans, we find at least two interesting Booleans (`httpd_enable_homedirs` and `httpd_read_user_content`):

   ```
   ~# sesearch -s httpd_t -t home_root_t -c dir -p open -AC
   Found 2 semantic av rules:
   DT allow httpd_t home_root_t : dir { getattr search open } ; [
   httpd_enable_homedirs ]
   DT allow httpd_t home_root_t : dir { getattr search open } ; [
   httpd_read_user_content ]
   ```

4. Let's first toggle `httpd_read_user_content`. This allows the web server to access all user files, which is functionally okay, but this also immediately grants it access to all files:

   ```
   ~# setsebool httpd_read_user_content on
   ```

5. Another approach (but this approach requires user intervention) is to have `~/public_html/` labeled as `httpd_user_content_t`. When this is done, `httpd_read_user_content` can be turned off and `httpd_enable_homedirs` can be enabled:

   ```
   ~$ chcon -R -t httpd_user_content_t public_html
   ```
   ```
   ~# setsebool httpd_read_user_content off
   ```
   ```
   ~# setsebool httpd_enable_homedirs on
   ```

6. When the changes are working nicely, we can persist the changes so that they survive a reboot:

   ```
   ~# setsebool -P httpd_enable_homedirs on
   ```

How it works...

The default web server policy in SELinux does not allow the web server to access user home content. If a vulnerability in a web application or the Apache web server itself would allow an attacker to read user content, SELinux will prevent this from happening. But, sometimes, user content access is needed.

By enabling the `httpd_read_user_content` Boolean, the web server domain (and all related domains) will have full read access to all user files. If users are not able (or do not know how) to set the proper context on their files, then this is the only suitable option.

A better approach, however, is to enable the `httpd_enable_homedirs` Boolean. This allows the web server search access through the home directory (`/home/user/`, which is labeled `user_home_dir_t`) but does not provide read access to user content (which is labeled `user_home_t`). Instead, the resources needed for the web server are labeled `httpd_user_content_t`—a type that regular users can relabel resources to (or relabel resources from). Next to `httpd_user_content_t`, one can also define the following content types:

 ▶ `httpd_user_htaccess_t` for the `.htaccess` files
 ▶ `httpd_user_script_exec_t` for user-provided CGI scripts
 ▶ `httpd_user_ra_content_t` for appendable resources (for the web server)
 ▶ `httpd_user_rw_content_t` for read/write resources (for the web server)

These resources can be set by the end user and give a finer control over how each resource within the `~/public_html/` location can be handled by the web server (and the web applications).

There's more...

Some SELinux supporting distributions have a daemon called `restorecond`, which can be used to automatically set the context of files the moment they are created/detected, without needing file transitions in policy. This can be used to automatically have `~/public_html/` labeled as `httpd_user_content_t`.

See also

▶ More information about per-user web directories can be found at `https://httpd.apache.org/docs/2.4/howto/public_html.html`

Assigning web content types

For standard web server configurations (without SELinux), access rights on resources for a web server are purely based on the ownership of the files (and the access mask applied to it). With SELinux, the resources can be labeled more specifically towards their functional meaning.

Web applications have content that should be read-only and content that should be read-write, but there are also specific types for resources such as `.htaccess` files. In this recipe, we'll look at the various web server content types and apply them to the right resources.

How to do it...

Execute the following steps to assign specific web content types to the right resources:

1. Take a look at the available content types for web servers by asking SELinux to show us all types that have the `httpdcontent` attribute set:

```
~$ seinfo -ahttpdcontent -x
  httpdcontent
    httpd_sys_content_t
    httpd_user_ra_content_t
    httpd_user_rw_content_t
    httpd_nagios_content_t
  ...
```

2. Query the existing policy for known context assignations (as those can give us pointers to what is still lacking):

```
~$ semanage fcontext -l | grep httpd_nagios
```

3. Now, assign the right context to those resources that aren't labeled correctly yet. The paths used here are an example for a Nagios installation:

```
~# semanage fcontext -a -t httpd_nagios_content_t /var/www/html/
nagios(/.*)?
```

```
~# semanage fcontext -a -t httpd_nagios_script_exec_t /usr/local/
lib/nagios/cgi-bin/.*
```

```
~# restorecon -R /var/www/html/nagios /usr/local/lib/nagios
```

How it works

The web server policy supports functional content types for web applications. These types are used for the following content types:

▶ Read-only content of the web application

▶ Writable content of the web application (for which a distinction is made between full writable content and content that can only be appended to, such as logfiles)

▶ Executable scripts (for CGI scripts and similar content)

The advantage is not so much that there is the distinction of read-only versus read-write, but that this is supported on a per-application basis, with types that are specific to one application. In the example, we looked at the content for the Nagios monitoring application.

This allows administrators to provide access to these resources towards specific applications or users. Even though all content in `/var/www/html/` might be owned by the Apache Linux user, we can still grant users (and applications) access to application-specific resources without needing to grant those users or applications full privileges on all Apache resources.

For the read-only content, there is the regular web application content (`httpd_nagios_content_t`) and the special `.htaccess` content (`httpd_nagios_htaccess_t`). The distinction is made primarily because access to the regular content is given more broadly (and depending on some SELinux Booleans, this can also become writable content), whereas the `.htaccess` content remains read-only.

To query the available web server content, we used the `httpdcontent` attribute. This attribute is assigned to all content, allowing administrators to create policies that govern all web content. The `httpdcontent` attribute is given to all these types, but there are also attributes called `httpd_rw_content`, `httpd_ra_content`, `httpd_htaccess_type`, and `httpd_script_exec_type` to allow for manipulation of those specific resources.

There's more...

We covered Nagios as an example web application, which has a set of web application related resources. Many other web applications or applications with web content have already been identified policy-wise.

On Linux distributions that have all known policies loaded by default, this overview will already be visible through the `seinfo` command as per our preceding example. If that isn't the case, we can always search through the SELinux policies to find out which modules call the `apache_content_template`—the interface that automatically generates the right web application content types:

```
~$ grep apache_content_template ${POLICY_LOCATION}/policy/modules/*/*.te
```

When different types become more troublesome than helpful, it is possible to ask the SELinux policy to see all those different types as just one common web content type and be done with it. This is supported through the `httpd_unified` Boolean. When this Boolean is enabled, the web server policy will treat all various web server resource types as one, unifying all the types. And, if the Booleans, `httpd_enable_cgi` and `httpd_builtin_scripting`, are enabled as well, then the web server domain has the privilege to execute that content as well.

Needless to say, unifying the web server resource contexts might make management simpler; it also increases the privileges of the web server domain towards various web resources, making it potentially less secure.

Using different web server ports

By default, web servers listen on the known web server ports (such as ports 80 and 443). Often, administrators might want to have the web server listen on a nondefault port. The SELinux policy might reject this, as it is not standard behavior for a web server to listen on other unrelated ports.

In this recipe, we will tell SELinux that a nondefault port should still be seen as a web server port.

How to do it...

In order to assign a label to a different port, execute the following steps:

1. To see all the ports that match `http_port_t`, use `semanage port -l`:

```
~# semanage port -l | grep -w http_port_t
http_port_t   tcp   80, 81, 443, 488, 8008, 8009, 8443, 9000
```

2. Query the SELinux policy to see which port type is assigned to a particular port. For instance, for port `8881`, the following command is used:

   ```
   ~$ seinfo --portcon=8881
   ```

3. If the port is identified as `unreserved_port_t`, then we can mark it as `http_port_t`:

   ```
   ~# semanage port -a -t http_port_t -p tcp 8881
   ```

4. If, however, the port has been already assigned a particular type, then we need to update the SELinux policy for the web server to allow it to listen on ports of this particular type. For instance, for port `9090` (`websm_port_t`), perform the following steps:

   1. First find the interface that allows binding on `websm_port_t`:

      ```
      ~$ sefindif websm_port_t.*bind
      ```

   2. Create a custom SELinux policy (`myhttpd`) with the following content:

      ```
      corenet_sendrecv_websm_server_packets(httpd_t)
      corenet_tcp_bind_websm_port(httpd_t)
      ```

   3. Load the policy to allow the web server to bind on the identified port type.

5. Finally, edit the web server configuration file to listen to the right port:

   ```
   Listen *:8881
   ```

How it works...

SELinux works with labels for all resources, including ports. In this example, we are looking at TCP port types to allow the web server to bind to.

With `seinfo`, we can see whether a port matches a known declaration. Ports with a value of `1024` or higher are, by default, labeled as `unreserved_port_t`, whereas, ports `511` or lower are labeled as `reserved_port_t` and those in between are labeled as `hi_reserved_port_t`. These are, however, defaults and more specific port types might be declared for a specific port.

If a port is not assigned a specific type yet, then we can assign one ourselves using `semanage port`. This is sufficient to allow the web server to bind to this port (there is no need for relabeling operations on ports, unlike files or directories, as this is done by the SELinux subsystem immediately).

If a port is already assigned a specific type, then it cannot be overridden by additional policies or the administrator. When this occurs, the SELinux policy will need to be enhanced to allow the web server to bind to this specific type.

In the example, we searched for the interface that would allow the web server to bind to the port, revealing `corenet_tcp_bind_websm_port` as the interface to use. However, we also added another interface—this is due to the way network controls are configured in SELinux, and may or may not be necessary on a system. The additional interface is `corenet_sendrecv_websm_server_packets`. This interface is used to allow the web server to send or receive packets labeled as `websm_server_packet_t`. Packet labeling allows for application-specific communication flow governance and extends the regular firewall capabilities of the Linux operating system (which focus primarily on network flow management) with SELinux domain awareness.

If packet labeling is needed, then packets are labeled through `iptables` on a local system, as shown in the following command:

```
~# iptables -t mangle -A INPUT -p tcp --dport 9090 -j SECMARK --selctx
system_u:object_r:websm_server_packet_t
```

If a system does not have such iptables-based labeling (known as SECMARK labeling), then the interface is not needed.

There's more...

Recent SELinux user space utilities have another command available to query the SELinux policy, called `sepolicy`. Searching for port declarations with `sepolicy` is done as follows:

```
~$ sepolicy network --port 8080

8080: tcp unreserved_port_t 1024-65535

8080: udp unreserved_port_t 1024-65535

8080: tcp http_cache_port_t 8080
```

Also, in the SELinux policy rules, we will notice that there is a third interface often enabled for network communication. In our example, the third interface would be called `corenet_tcp_sendrecv_websm_port`. This access vector would enable the domain to send and receive messages on the `websm_port_t` TCP socket. However, the support for this access vector has been disabled in recent policies in favor of SECMARK labeling.

See also

> ▸ SECMARK labeling is explored in *Chapter 9, Aligning SELinux with DAC*

Using custom content types

Next up is to create our own set of content types for a web application that does not have a policy associated with it yet. We will use **DokuWiki** (available at `https://www.dokuwiki.org`) as an example.

Getting ready

Install DokuWiki either through the Linux distributions' package manager or manually through a downloaded release from the main site. In this example, we assume that DokuWiki is installed at `/srv/web/dokuwiki/`.

How to do it...

To use custom web content types, follow the next set of steps:

1. Create a policy called `mydokuwiki.te` with the following content:

   ```
   apache_content_template(dokuwiki)
   ```

2. Add a file context definition file called `mydokuwiki.fc`, which contains the following code:

   ```
   /srv/web/dokuwiki/lib/plugins(/.*)?
     gen_context(system_u:object_r:httpd_dokuwiki_rw_content_t,s0)
   /srv/web/dokuwiki/conf(/.*)?
     gen_context(system_u:object_r:httpd_dokuwiki_rw_content_t,s0)
   /srv/web/dokuwiki/data(/.*)?
     gen_context(system_u:object_r:httpd_dokuwiki_rw_content_t,s0)
   /srv/web/dokuwiki/data/\.htaccess  --
     gen_context(system_u:object_r:httpd_dokuwiki_htaccess_t,s0)
   /srv/web/dokuwiki(/.*)?
     gen_context(system_u:object_r:httpd_dokuwiki_content_t,s0)
   ```

3. Build and load the policy and then relabel all DokuWiki files using the following commands:

   ```
   ~# semodule -i mydokuwiki.pp
   ~# restorecon -RvF /srv/web/dokuwiki
   ```

How it works...

All the magic associated with creating web application content in SELinux is handled by the `apache_content_template` interface. With `seshowif`, one can show all underlying SELinux policy rules as follows:

▸ Various SELinux types are created, such as `httpd_dokuwiki_content_t` and the like, and the proper attributes are assigned to it (such as the `httpdcontent` attribute).

▸ An SELinux Boolean is created, which allows the administrator to enable or disable the web application to write to public files (labeled as `public_content_rw_t`). This is an SELinux type used for resources that are shared across multiple services (such as FTP servers, web servers, and many more).

> ▶ The necessary privileges are granted to the web server domain to access and handle the newly defined types, as well as enabling CGI domains for the web application. For our DokuWiki example, this is not needed as everything is handled by the PHP code parsed and executed by the web server itself (usually).

We then labeled all DokuWiki files accordingly, based on the DokuWiki best practices for file access. Some administrators might want to have the `conf/` subdirectory labeled as a nonwritable resource, and only (temporarily) enable this during the configuration. Although this is a valid approach, it might be sufficient to use Linux DAC file access controls to accomplish the same results.

There's more...

Using the `apache_content_template` interface is a simple way to create web content types, but it has the downside that it is an all-or-nothing approach, and the module now heavily depends on the web server module (`apache`).

Experienced users might want to selectively create content and assign the right attributes to it, allowing the web server domain to interact with the resources while still keeping granular control over the types and resources.

We'll leave this as an exercise that you can do to see how this can be accomplished.

Creating a custom CGI domain

Sometimes, it might not be necessary to create a full set of types. Consider a CGI script that is triggered but without the need for a specific set of content types. Sure, one can mark the script as `httpd_sys_script_exec_t` (if it is a system's CGI script) or `httpd_user_script_exec_t` (if it is a user's custom CGI script) so that the resulting script runs in the `httpd_sys_script_t` or `httpd_user_script_t` domain.

But, if those domains do not hold enough privileges (or too many privileges), it might be wise to create a custom CGI domain instead.

How to do it...

To create a custom CGI domain, the following approach can be used:

1. Create a custom SELinux policy module (`mycgiscript.te`) with the following content:
```
policy_module(mycgiscript, 0.1)
type cgiscript_t;
type cgiscript_exec_t;
```

```
domain_type(cgiscript_t)
domain_entry_file(cgiscript_t, cgiscript_exec_t)
apache_cgi_domain(cgiscript_t, cgiscript_exec_t)
```

2. Create the proper file context file (`mycgiscript.fc`), marking the executable as `cgiscript_exec_t`:

```
/path/to/script   --
  gen_context(system_u:object_r:cgiscript_exec_t,s0)
```

3. Build and load the module.

4. Relabel the executable and test it out:

   ~# restorecon /path/to/script

5. As the `cgiscript_t` domain is primitive in its rights, the script will most likely not work—however, do not turn SELinux in permissive mode. The audit logs will show the access attempts that were denied. Instead of using `audit2allow` to automatically grant everything, use the `sefindif` function to find a proper interface. Add the right interfaces to the module and retry until the script works properly.

How it works...

The policy module defines a domain type (`cgiscript_t`) and an executable type (`cgiscript_exec_t`). With the `domain_type` interface, `cgiscript_t` is marked as a domain (and the proper SELinux rules to deal with this new domain are created as well). With `domain_entry_type`, the SELinux policy is updated to mark `cgiscript_exec_t` as the type that can be used to transition towards the `cgiscript_t` domain.

Then, we call `apache_cgi_domain`, which allows the web server domain (`httpd_t`) to execute the `cgiscript_exec_t` labeled resources and have the resulting process run in the `cgiscript_t` domain.

The initial policy module, however, is very primitive and will not hold enough privileges. It is a matter of trial and error to update the policy. For instance, consider that the script calls a binary; the audit logs might show the following content:

```
type=AVC msg=audit(1363205612.277:476924): avc: denied { execute }
    for pid=6855 comm="cgiscript.pl" name="perl" dev=sda3 ino=4325828
scontext=system_u:system_r:cgiscript_t:s0
    tcontext=system_u:object_r:bin_t:s0 tclass=file
```

To find out which policy interface would allow this, we can use `sefindif` again:

~$ sefindif exec.*bin_t'

interface(\`corecmd_exec_bin',\`

** can_exec($1, bin_t)**

Developing custom policies remains a trial-and-error approach, but this is the only method available, which ensures that only necessary privileges are granted to a domain. Some policy developers would suggest to turn on the permissive mode and look through all denials in the audit logs. The problem with that approach is that these denials might not lead to the right SELinux policy rules.

For instance, the script might need to call another executable (and transition to a domain). In permissive mode, the transition will not occur, and it would look like the main domain (cgiscript_t) needs all privileges that the target command needs—even though all that is needed is a proper domain transition.

By focusing on the enforcing mode, we can gradually increase the policy while keeping the *least privilege* principle in place, only allowing those privileges that are actually needed.

Setting up mod_selinux

In the next set of recipes, we use an Apache module called mod_selinux to make Apache SELinux-aware and to support configurable transitions. In other words, the context in which Apache is running is no longer a statically defined context, but can be changed according to the administrators' needs.

In this recipe, we will install mod_selinux from its source as many Linux distributions do not offer it by default, even though it is a very powerful addition to the web server (which is also why support for mod_selinux is often called Apache/SELinux Plus).

How to do it...

You can set up mod_selinux through the following steps:

1. Download the sources from https://github.com/kaigai/mod_selinux.
2. Make sure that the Apache development headers (httpd-devel on Red Hat or Fedora systems) are installed.
3. Build and install the mod_selinux shared library for Apache using apxs:

   ```
   ~# apxs -c -i mod_selinux.c
   ```

 It may be possible that the build fails with an error about client_ip. If that is the case, edit mod_selinux.c at the line number shown in the error and use remote_ip instead of client_ip, after which the apxs command can be run again.

4. Build and install the `mod_selinux` SELinux policy module, whose files are also part of the downloaded sources:

   ```
   ~$ cp mod_selinux.te ${DEVROOT}/local
   ~$ cp mod_selinux.if ${DEVROOT}/local
   ~$ cd ${DEVROOT}/local && make mod_selinux.pp
   ~# semodule -i mod_selinux.pp
   ```

5. Edit the web server configuration (`httpd.conf`) and add in the proper `LoadModule` line:

   ```
   LoadModule selinux_module modules/mod_selinux.so
   ```

6. Restart the web server. Its logfiles should tell you that the SELinux policy support is loaded:

   ```
   [Fri Apr 18 13:11:23 2014] [notice] SELinux policy enabled;
   httpd running as context unconfined_u:system_r:httpd_t:s0-s0:c0.
   c1023
   ```

How it works...

The `mod_selinux.c` file contains the Apache module code and can be built using apxs—the Apache eXtenSion tool. This tool will perform the following tasks:

▶ Call the compiler with the proper arguments to build a dynamic shared object that can be loaded at runtime by the Apache web server

▶ Install the resulting module in the proper Apache `modules/` directory

The build failure mentioned in the recipe can come up depending on the Apache version in use, where a variable has a different name (`client_ip` instead of `remote_ip`).

Next, we copied and deployed the `mod_selinux` SELinux policy just like we did with other SELinux policy modules.

Finally, the web server is updated to enable the `mod_selinux` Apache module. With the `mod_selinux` shared library in place, Apache is now ready to make SELinux-related decisions.

If the `mod_selinux` support has to be distributed to multiple systems, then only the `mod_selinux.so` (now installed in the web server `modules/` directory, such as `/usr/lib64/httpd/modules/`) and `mod_selinux.pp` files (the SELinux policy module) need to be distributed.

See also

▶ A good write-up on `mod_selinux` can be found at `http://code.google.com/p/sepgsql/wiki/Apache_SELinux_plus`

Starting Apache with limited clearance

In the previous chapter, we manipulated the `/etc/rc.d/init.d/httpd` init script to use `runcon` in order for the web server to run with a limited clearance. But with the help of `mod_selinux`, this can be made configurable.

How to do it...

In order to start Apache with limited security clearance, follow the given steps:

1. Edit the Apache web server configuration file (`httpd.conf`) and add in the following code:

```
<IfModule mod_selinux.c>
  selinuxServerDomain *:s0-s0:c0.c10
</IfModule>
```

2. Undo the changes made to the service script in the previous chapter.

3. Restart the web server and confirm that it is running with the `s0-s0:c0.c10` clearance by issuing the following commands:

```
~# /etc/rc.d/init.d/httpd restart
~# ps -efZ | grep httpd
system_u:system_r:httpd_t:s0-s0:c0.c10 root 2838 1  0 13:14 ?
00:00:00 /usr/sbin/httpd
system_u:system_r:httpd_t:s0-s0:c0.c10 apache 2840 2838  0
13:14 ? 00:00:00 /usr/sbin/httpd
```

How it works...

As mentioned before, with `mod_selinux`, the Apache web server becomes SELinux-aware, meaning it can alter its own behavior and interact with the SELinux subsystem based on configuration settings as well as SELinux policy rules.

With the `selinuxServerDomain` configuration directive, `mod_selinux` performs a dynamic change of the current context to a new context, which is called a dynamic domain transition or dynamic range transition (it is called domain if the type changes, range if the sensitivity level or security clearance changes). This is only possible if an application is SELinux-aware.

Now, such a transition is still governed through SELinux policies. For instance, the range to which the Apache web server can transition must be dominated by the range the Apache web server originally has (which was `s0-s0:c0.c1024` in our example).

The mod_selinux module does not support lookups on the context, making it impossible to use human-readable sensitivities (governed through mcstransd as we've seen previously).

There's more...

It is possible to define different types, allowing the entire web server to run in a custom domain. For this to happen, the httpd_t domain must have the rights to dynamically transition to the target type (the dyntransition permission in the process class). Then, the selinuxServerDomain call could look like the following code:

```
selinuxServerDomain myhttpd_t:s0-s0:c0.c10
```

Of course, many more privileges are needed as well in order to access resources already accessible by the httpd_t domain at startup, but the dyntransition permission is specific to the SELinux-aware applications that want to support dynamic domain transitions instead of transitioning upon process execution.

Mapping HTTP users to contexts

Applications generally run with a static context, which inhibits all privileges that are needed for the application. Even services (daemons) generally stay within their own context during the entire life cycle of the service. But, with mod_selinux, it is possible to transition the context of the web server handler (the process or thread responsible for handling a specific request) to another context based on the authenticated user. This allows the administrator to grant certain privileges to the application based on the user. When a lower-privileged user abuses a vulnerability in the web application, then the reduced privileges on the web application itself might prevent a successful exploit.

How to do it...

Through the following set of steps, we will map a web user to a specific SELinux context:

1. Create a mapping file in which the users are listed together with their target context. For instance, to have user John's requests handled with the sensitivity s0:c0,c2, user Cindy's requests with the sensitivity s0:c0.c5,c7, all unauthenticated users as anon_webapp_t:s0, and the other authenticated users as user_ webapp_t:s0:c0:

```
john        *:s0:c0,c2
cindy       *:s0:c0.c5,c7
__anonymous__    anon_webapp_t:s0
*           user_webapp_t:s0:c0
```

2. Save this file on a web server-readable location, such as `/etc/httpd/conf/mod_selinux.map`.

3. Edit the web server configuration file and add in the following line:

```
selinuxDomainMap    /etc/httpd/conf/mod_selinux.map
```

4. Restart the web server.

How it works...

The `mod_selinux` module is aware of the authenticated user value and, based on the settings in the mappings file, it can transition the request handler to a smaller sensitivity range (as is the case in the first two examples) or to different domains altogether.

There is an important constraint to this though. The target context to which the handler can transition must be bound by the main type (`httpd_t`). This means that the permissions granted to the target context must be a subset of the permissions granted to `httpd_t`. This is performed through the `typebounds` statement, as follows:

```
typebounds httpd_t anon_webapp_t;
```

This is because web server handlers are usually threads (or lightweight processes) instead of processes. Threads share a lot of resources, often in ways that SELinux cannot manage. As a result, if one thread gains more rights than the web server, then the secure state of the web server (as a whole) might be in jeopardy. Also, the information flow between different contexts would be difficult, if not impossible to govern.

Using source address mapping to decide on contexts

The `mod_selinux` Apache module has access to other information than just the username (in case of authenticated users). It can access environment variables (which are used in the Apache web configuration through the `SetEnvIf` directives), allowing a very flexible approach on SELinux context handling within the application.

In this recipe, we will use this to change the context of request handlers based on the remote IP address of the client.

How to do it...

Alongside web users, we can also use source address information to decide on the context. This is done by completing the following steps:

1. First, we define the `TARGETDOMAIN` environment variable based on the remote IP address in the web server configuration (`httpd.conf`):

```
SetEnvIf Remote_Addr "10\.0\.[0-9]+\.[0-9]+$"
   TARGETDOMAIN=user_webapp_t:s0
SetEnvIf Remote_Addr "10\.1\.[0-9]+\.[0-9]+$"
   TARGETDOMAIN=anon_webapp_t:s0
SetEnvIf TARGETDOMAIN ^$ TARGETDOMAIN=*:s0
```

2. Then, in the same web server configuration, we invoke the `selinuxDomainEnv` directive, which will have the handler context transitioned to the value inside `TARGETDOMAIN`:

   ```
   selinuxDomainEnv TARGETDOMAIN
   ```

3. Restart the web server for the changes to take effect.

How it works...

In the first step, we used Apache's `SetEnvIf` directive (provided through `mod_setenvif`) to check the remote IP address of the client (`Remote_Addr`). If it matches the expression given, then we set the `TARGETDOMAIN` variable to the given context. In our example, we used a different type for each match, but it is also possible to just change the security clearance. We finished with a check that verified if the `TARGETDOMAIN` variable has been set. If not, then a default value (`*:s0`) is assigned.

Next, we called the `selinuxDomainEnv` directive, which makes a transition to the domain provided in the `TARGETDOMAIN` variable.

There's more...

The example uses `Remote_Addr`, but many other request-related aspects can be used:

  ▶ With `Remote_Host`, the hostname of the client can be queried and used to make decisions.
  ▶ With `Server_Addr`, the address of the web server itself (on which the request was received) can be used. This is useful in a multihomed system, where the web server binds to all available IP addresses.
  ▶ With `Request_Method`, the type of request (such as `GET` or `POST`) can be used.
  ▶ With `Request_Protocol`, the name and version of the HTTP protocol (such as `HTTP/1.0` or `HTTP/1.1`) can be used.
  ▶ With `Request_URI`, the request URL can be used to tune the context or clearance.

See also

  ▶ For more information about Apache's `mod_setenvif` support, consult the module documentation at `http://httpd.apache.org/docs/2.4/mod/mod_setenvif.html`

Separating virtual hosts with mod_selinux

One of Apache's strengths is that it can differentiate sites based on the name used to connect to the server, rather than just the IP address, port, and URL. This is called virtual host support and is a very popular approach to multitenant website and web application hosting.

For instance, a web server running on a single IP address can still host the sites of multiple customers, say `www.companyX.com` and `www.companyY.com`. With `mod_selinux`, we can change the context or security clearance of the web server request handlers based on the associated virtual host.

How to do it...

The following approach distinguishes virtual host confinement through `mod_selinux`:

1. Decide on the contexts for the individual tenants. In the previous chapter, we used `s0:c100` for company X and `s0:c101` for company Y.

2. In each virtual host, set the right clearance. For instance, for company X set the clearance as follows:

```
<VirtualHost *:443>
   ServerName www.companyX.com
   selinuxDomainVal *:s0-s0:c100
</VirtualHost>
```

3. Restart the web server for the changes to take effect.

How it works...

Unlike the `selinuxServerDomain` directive, which is for the entire web server, the `selinuxDomainVal` directive sets the context of the handlers (virtual hosts) individually. As we covered in the previous chapter, using multiple categories for a multitenant system is a flexible way of dealing with information isolation between tenants.

An important difference with the previous chapter, however, is that the `mod_selinux` module does not use `mcstransd`. The following setting will fail:

```
selinuxDomainVal *:CompanyXClearance
```

Such a setting would result in the following error message by Apache:

```
[error] (22)Invalid argument: SELinux:
setcon_raw("unconfined_u:system_r:httpd_t:CompanyXClearance")
failed
```

As such, we need to use the standard sensitivity notation.

See also

- You can find more information about Apache virtual host support at `http://httpd.apache.org/docs/2.4/vhosts/`

4

Creating a Desktop Application Policy

In this chapter, we will cover the following topics:

- ▸ Researching the application's logical design
- ▸ Creating a skeleton policy
- ▸ Setting context definitions
- ▸ Defining application role interfaces
- ▸ Testing and enhancing the policy
- ▸ Ignoring permissions we don't need
- ▸ Creating application resource interfaces
- ▸ Adding conditional policy rules
- ▸ Adding build-time policy decisions

Introduction

Up until now, we've modified and enhanced existing policies and interacted with the SELinux subsystem through the available administrative commands. But, in order to truly benefit from the protection measures that SELinux provides, we need to create our own policies for applications that would otherwise run with either too many privileges, or not run at all.

Desktop applications are a good example. The end user domains (`unconfined_t` for policies which support unconfined domains, and `user_t`, `staff_t`, and the like for the other policies) have many privileges assigned to them to allow generic applications to be executed while remaining in the user domain.

This has a huge downside: vulnerabilities within desktop applications or malfunctioning applications can create havoc with the users' files and resources, potentially exposing information to malicious users. If all end user applications run within the same domain, then we cannot talk about a least privilege environment. After all, this single user domain then has to have the sum of all privileges needed by various applications.

In this chapter, we will create a desktop application policy for Microsoft Skype™, a popular text messaging, voice, and video call application, which also runs on Linux systems, but is proprietary and thus its code cannot be reviewed to find what it might do. Confining this application ensures that the application can only perform the actions we allow it to do.

Researching the application's logical design

Before embarking on a policy development spree, we need to look at the application's behavior and logical design. We will get to know the application and its interactions as we begin to model this into the SELinux policy.

How to do it...

To prepare an SELinux policy for the application, let's first look at how the application behaves:

1. Look into the files and directories that the application will interact with and write down the privileges that the application needs. Try to structure access based on the functionalities of the application.

2. Figure out which network resources are required by the application, which ports does the application bind (listen) to (if any), and which ports does it need to connect to.

3. If the application needs to interact with other SELinux domains (processes), how does this interaction look (or what is it for)?

4. Does the application require specific hardware access or other kernel-provided resources?

How it works...

Gathering information on at least these four resources (files, network, applications, and hardware/kernel) helps us to start with a skeleton policy file. In the end, we might have a schematic representation of these resources, as shown in the following diagram:

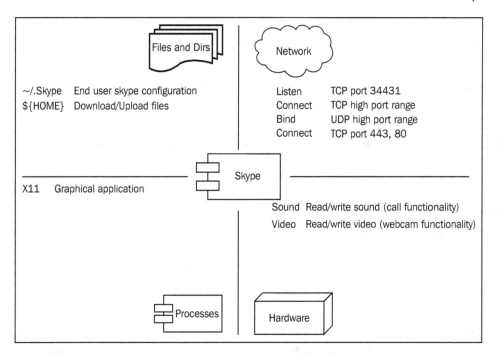

Let's look at how this works out for our example.

Files and directories

There are three main file accesses needed for the Skype™ application.

The first is its own, user-specific configuration, which is stored at ~/.Skype/. This will contain all settings for the application, including contact list, chat history, and more. In SELinux, user-specific configuration entries are labeled as *_home_t and marked as user home content, allowing the end user to still manage these resources.

The second consists of the generic user files, which our application needs access to in order to upload or download files. This can be any end user file, although some distributions create specific support for this (such as through a ~/Downloads/ location).

The third consists of the general resources of the Unix system that are available for the application. This access is needed for the application to load the necessary libraries. During application policy development, this is often not mentioned, as it is a default access provided to all applications.

Network resources

The application needs to interact with network resources through its messaging, voice, and video chat functionality.

In general, we know that the application needs to connect to the central Skype™ infrastructure for all centrally managed services, such as authentication, directory searches, and more. This connection will be through TCP.

Next to the central infrastructure, the application will also connect to the Skype™ instances of other users for direct communication. This connection will be through both TCP and UDP (as UDP is more common for video and voice).

Processes

As the application is a graphical application, we know that it needs to interact with the X11 server running on the workstation. As we will see in the recipes in this chapter, this automatically requires a set of types and permissions to be assigned to the application.

Other than that, there are no specific interactions with other domains.

Hardware and kernel resources

Finally, on the hardware level, the application will need access to the video and sound devices (for the webcam and voice call functionality, respectively).

The application will also need to use the user terminals in case of errors (so that the error message can be displayed).

Creating a skeleton policy

With the logical setup now in place, we can draft a skeleton policy. This policy will be a translation from the logical setup we encountered to SELinux policy rules.

The entire policy is written in a `myskype.te` file. The final result of this set of recipes is also available through the download pack of this book as a reference.

How to do it...

We start with a base skeleton that we can enhance later. This skeleton is developed as follows:

1. We start with the declaration of the various types. From the design, we can deduce four types:

   - `skype_t` as the main process domain
   - `skype_exec_t` as the label for the Skype executable(s)

- ❑ `skype_home_t` for the user configuration files and directories of the `skype_t` domain

- ❑ `skype_tmpfs_t` is needed for shared memory and the X11 interaction

The code to deduce these four types is as follows:

```
policy_module(myskype, 0.1)

attribute_role skype_roles;

type skype_t;
type skype_exec_t;
userdom_user_application_domain(skype_t, skype_exec_t)
role skype_roles types skype_t;

type skype_home_t;
userdom_user_home_content(skype_home_t)

type skype_tmpfs_t;
userdom_user_tmpfs_file(skype_tmpfs_t);
```

2. Next, we write up the policy rules for accessing the various types, starting with the manage rights on `~/.Skype/`:

```
# Allow manage rights on ~/.Skype
manage_dirs_pattern(skype_t, skype_home_t, skype_home_t)
manage_files_pattern(skype_t, skype_home_t, skype_home_t)
userdom_user_home_dir_filetrans(skype_t, skype_home_t, dir,
   ".Skype")
```

3. We enable the X11 access and shared memory. This is a common set of privileges that need to be assigned to X11-enabled applications:

```
# Shared memory (also needed for X11)
manage_files_pattern(skype_t, skype_tmpfs_t, skype_tmpfs_t)
manage_lnk_files_pattern(skype_t, skype_tmpfs_t,
   skype_tmpfs_t)
manage_fifo_files_pattern(skype_t, skype_tmpfs_t,
   skype_tmpfs_t)
manage_sock_files_pattern(skype_t, skype_tmpfs_t,
   skype_tmpfs_t)
fs_tmpfs_filetrans(skype_t, skype_tmpfs_t, { file lnk_file fifo_
file sock_file })

# Application is an X11 application
xserver_user_x_domain_template(skype, skype_t,
   skype_tmpfs_t)
```

4. Next, we write down the network access rules, as follows:

```
# Network access
corenet_tcp_bind_generic_node(skype_t)
corenet_udp_bind_generic_node(skype_t)
# Central skype services
corenet_tcp_connect_http_port(skype_t)
corenet_tcp_connect_all_unreserved_ports(skype_t)
# Listen for incoming communication
corenet_tcp_bind_all_unreserved_ports(skype_t)
corenet_udp_bind_all_unreserved_ports(skype_t)
```

5. Finally, we have the device accesses:

```
# Voice and video calls
dev_read_sound(skype_t)
dev_read_video_dev(skype_t)
dev_write_sound(skype_t)
dev_write_video_dev(skype_t)
# Terminal (tty) output
userdom_use_user_terminals(skype_t)
```

How it works...

In the skeleton policy, we start with the SELinux policy rules that we know will be necessary. If we are somewhat uncertain about one or more rules, it is perfectly fine to comment them out for starters and enable those as we move on to the testing phase in the *Testing and enhancing the policy* recipe later.

The skeleton starts off with the type declarations, which focus on the resources of the application. We then enhance the application domain with the proper privileges towards these resources. After the resource access, we look at the X11 privileges and finish with the network interaction of the application.

Type declarations

The first part of any policy is the declaration of types and roles. We first create a role attribute called `skype_roles` to which the `skype_t` SELinux domain is granted. This role attribute will then be assigned to the users who are allowed to call the application. Next, we list the various SELinux types that the policy will provide and also give those types a specific meaning. For instance, the `skype_t` and `skype_exec_t` types are given the proper meaning through the `userdom_user_application_domain` template. This template looks like the following:

```
interface(`userdom_user_application_domain',`
        application_domain($1, $2)
        ubac_constrained($1)
')
```

The `application_domain` template, which is called from within `userdom_user_ application_domain`, has the following definition:

```
interface(`application_domain',`
        application_type($1)
        application_executable_file($2)
        domain_entry_file($1, $2)
')
```

This results in the `skype_t` domain to be marked as an application type (a true domain), whereas `skype_exec_t` is an executable file, which can be used as an entry point to the `skype_t` domain. Finally, `skype_t` is marked as `ubac_constrained`, which is used in case of **User-based access control** (**UBAC**), where access to resources is not only governed through the types and its access vectors, but also through the SELinux user. In other words, if the SELinux user, `userX_u`, would somehow be able to access the processes of another SELinux user (`userY_u`), then the `skype_t` domain will not be reachable as the UBAC constraints would come in action, preventing any interaction between the two.

All `userdom_user_*` templates mark the associated resources as UBAC constrained, together with the true file type association, so `userdom_user_tmpfs_file` marks the file not only as a `tmpfs_t` file (the type used for shared memory), but also makes it UBAC constrained.

Managing files and directories

Next, we provide the access rights to files and resources. In the example, we limit access to `~/.Skype/` only and automatically mark `~/.Skype/` as `skype_home_t` when it is created inside a user home directory (through `userdom_user_home_dir_filetrans`), even though we identified the need to manage user content files as well. This is because we need to make a policy design decision here—do we want the application to have full access to all user resources or would we rather limit the access? And inversely, do we want other applications that can access user content to access Skype™ user (configuration) data?

If we do not want the application to access any user content, then we do not need to add any rules: the policy will only allow search rights through the user home directory (in order to locate `~/.Skype/`) and deny everything else.

If we would like to grant the application access to the user content, we can add in the following calls:

```
userdom_manage_user_home_content_files(skype_t)
userdom_manage_user_home_content_dirs(skype_t)
```

This will grant full manage rights on user files and directories to the `skype_t` domain.

In the Gentoo Linux policy, additional types have been made available to provide a finer-grained access control to user files. These types map to the **XDG Base Directory Specification** (**XDGBDS**) as provided by the Free Desktop community, and include the `xdg_downloads_home_t` type. End users can mark files and directories as `xdg_downloads_home_t` and allow applications to have selective access to user files, without risking that these applications have access to the more private files of that user.

In Gentoo, this means that the following call can be added to the policy:

```
xdg_manage_downloads_home(skype_t)
```

X11 and shared memory

When an application needs to interact with the X11 server (as a client application), much of this interaction is done through shared memory. In Linux, shared memory can be interpreted as files on a tmpfs mount (think `/dev/shm/`) although other shared memory constructions are still possible without tmpfs.

In SELinux, policy developers want to make sure that this shared memory is labeled specifically for the domain. For this, they create a type with `_tmpfs_t` as the suffix. In our example, this is `skype_tmpfs_t`. Of course, we need to grant manage rights on the shared memory (for all classes that will be used) to the `skype_t` domain. In case of X11 interaction, these are files, symbolic links, FIFOs, and sockets.

Next to the manage rights, we also include a file transition: whenever `skype_t` creates a file, symbolic link, FIFO, or socket in a `tmpfs_t` labeled location, then this resource should be automatically labeled `skype_tmpfs_t`. This is done through the `fs_tmpfs_filetrans` call.

Finally, we use `xserver_user_x_domain_template` that contains all the SELinux privileges necessary for both the X11 client as well as X11 server to interact with each other. This template uses a prefix argument (the first argument, which we provided as `skype`), which will be used to create an X11 resource type called `skype_input_xevent_t`. Similar to what we've seen for web servers (where an `apache_content_template` call was used), this template gives an easy approach to automatically build additional types and enable the X11 support.

Next to the prefix, the domain itself is passed (`skype_t`) and the label used for the shared memory (`skype_tmpfs_t`) are passed on as those are needed for the X11 server support.

The network access

For the network access, we start by providing the `skype_t` domain with bind privileges on a TCP socket and its IP address (which is represented by `node_t`).

Next, we allow the `skype_t` domain to connect to the central Skype™ services, which are available on HTTPS port `443` (authentication) and various seemingly random high TCP ports (network nodes). The HTTP target port is identified as an `http_port_t` type, the others are for the unreserved ports.

Finally, we allow the `skype_t` domain to listen for incoming communications. By default, this is on a high TCP port for messages and state information, while for voice and video chat, this is through UDP.

A simple way to identify the necessary types is to look at the `netstat` output, as it shows us what ports a process is listening on, the protocol family (TCP or UDP), as well as which ports it is connecting to:

```
~$ netstat -naput | grep skype
tcp  0   0 0.0.0.0:34431  0.0.0.0:*  LISTEN  8160/skype
tcp  0   0 10.221.44.241:40650  111.221.77.150:40008  ESTABLISHED  8160/
skype
...
udp  0   0 0.0.0.0:34302  0.0.0.0:*     8160/skype
```

There's more...

The access to the sound and video devices is trivial, but during the design, it is very well possible that many more accesses are already identified (as ours is just an example). As we continue developing policies, writing a skeleton policy will become more trivial.

A great source for learning more about the policies is to look for an existing policy of a similar application, or an application that has certain functionalities that resemble the functionalities offered by the application we're writing a policy for. For Skype™, we could look at the policy of Gift (a peer-to-peer file sharing application), which is an end user, graphical application with peer-to-peer communication flows, supporting uploading and downloading files.

After all, SELinux policies are a write-down of what the expected behavior is of a domain. If another application has the same or similar behavior, then its policy will be very similar too.

In the previous example, we grouped the permissions together based on the functional need. However, the coding style for SELinux policy files, as mentioned by the reference policy, uses a different grouping, so make sure that if the policy would be sent upstream, this coding style is followed instead.

See also

▶ For more information about the XDGBDS, see `http://standards.freedesktop.org/basedir-spec/latest/`

Setting context definitions

The next step in the policy development is to mark its resources with the proper file contexts. This will label the files of the application correctly, making sure that the SELinux policy makes the right decisions.

How to do it...

To update the file context definitions, follow the next set of steps:

1. Create the `myskype.fc` file and add in the definition for `~/.Skype/`:

   ```
   HOME_DIR/\.Skype(/.*)?  gen_context(system_u:object_r:skype_
   home_t,s0)
   ```

2. Next, add in the definitions for the `skype` binaries:

   ```
   /opt/skype/skype   --  gen_context(system_u:object_r:skype_
                          exec_t,s0)
   /opt/bin/skype   --  gen_context(system_u:object_r:skype_exec_t,s0)
   /usr/bin/skype   --  gen_context(system_u:object_r:skype_exec_t,s0)
   ```

How it works...

The definitions for the binaries are standard, path-based context declarations. The one for the user home directory, however, is special.

As can be seen from the example, the path starts with HOME_DIR. This is a special variable used by SELinux libraries, which automatically maps to all Linux users' home directories. Rather than creating a `/home/[^/]*/\.Skype(/.*)?` context directly, which has the design problem that home directories on other locations (such as `/export/home/user/`) will not match, the SELinux libraries will check the home directories of all real users (with a user ID starting at `500`, although this is configurable) and for each different home root directory (`/home/` is the most commonly used one), it will generate the proper contexts.

The result of this operation is stored as the `file_contexts.homedirs` file inside `/etc/selinux/mcs/contexts/files/` and is automatically created during policy build (through the `genhomedircon` command).

Next to HOME_DIR, other supported variables are HOME_ROOT (which represents the home root path) and ROLE (which is the first role associated with a user).

Defining application role interfaces

Finally, before testing the policy, we need to create a role interface and assign it to the user domain that will be used to test (and run) the application. If we don't create a role interface and assign it to a user domain, then the user domain will either have no privileges to execute the application at all, or the application will run with the user context rather than the newly defined skype_t domain. If the user domain isn't unconfined, then chances are that the application will fail.

How to do it...

Role interfaces are the gateways of a policy. They ensure that domains and SELinux users can interact with the application and that the set of privileges for a particular application are coherent.

We create such an interface in the .if file and then assign this interface to a user domain in order to test the interface:

1. Create the myskype.if file with the following interface in it:

```
interface(`skype_role',`
  gen_require(`
    type skype_t, skype_exec_t, skype_tmp_t, skype_home_t;
  ')
  # Allow the skype_t domain for the user role
  roleattribute $1 skype_roles;
  # Allow domain transition for user domain to skype_t
  domtrans_pattern($2, skype_exec_t, skype_t)
  # Interact with skype process
  ps_process_pattern($2, skype_t)
  allow $2 skype_t:process { ptrace signal_perms };
  # Manage skype file resources
  manage_dirs_pattern($2, skype_home_t, skype_home_t)
  manage_files_pattern($2, skype_home_t, skype_home_t)
  manage_lnk_files_pattern($2, skype_home_t, skype_home_t)
  # Allow user to relabel the resources if needed
  relabel_dirs_pattern($2, skype_home_t, skype_home_t)
  relabel_files_pattern($2, skype_home_t, skype_home_t)
  relabel_lnk_files_pattern($2, skype_home_t, skype_home_t)
')
```

2. Create a policy for the user domain (for instance, `myunprivuser.te`) that grants regular users access to the `skype_t` domain, by assigning the user domain the `skype_role` call:

```
policy_module(myunprivuser, 1.0)
gen_require(`
  type user_t;
  role user_r;
')
optional_policy(`
  skype_role(user_r, user_t)
')
```

3. Build both policies and load them. Then, relabel the `skype` binary files (and possibly preexisting ~/.Skype/ locations):

```
~# restorecon /opt/skype/bin/skype /opt/bin/skype /usr/bin/skype
~# restorecon -RF /home/user/.Skype
```

How it works...

Although we have defined all the rules for the `skype_t` domain that we think are needed (in the next recipe, the policy will be extended until it really works), we have not defined the rules yet to allow a user domain to actually execute the `skype_exec_t` binaries and have the process run in the `skype_t` domain.

To accomplish that, we need to ensure that a domain transition occurs to the `skype_t` domain when the user executes `skype_exec_t`. This is handled by the `domtrans_pattern` call. But before we allow the domain transition, we first need to allow the `skype_t` domain for the user role, which is done through the `roleattribute` call.

Until now, we focused primarily on type enforcement rules (that is, granting privileges to SELinux domains based on the label of the target resource). In order to allow certain users to run an application, the application domain itself needs to be granted to the user role. This is supported through SELinux's **role-based access control (RBAC)** model. This RBAC model ensures that a certain domain (`skype_t`, in our example) can only be used by the roles we configure it for (`user_r`, in our example). Other roles, such as DBA roles (`dbadm_r`) might have no need for running the Skype™ application, so they will not be granted access to the `skype_t` domain.

Not granting a domain does not necessarily prevent the application from executing within the user domain itself. To accomplish that, we need to make sure that the executable file type cannot be executed by other roles. Instead of using `userdom_user_application_domain` for the `skype_t` and `skype_exec_t` types (which would assign a generic executable attribute to the `skype_exec_t` type), we would use something similar to the following:

```
application_type(skype_t)
files_type(skype_exec_t)
allow skype_t skype_exec_t:file { entrypoint mmap_file_
perms ioctl lock };
ubac_constrained(skype_t)
```

As the user domain, which needs to be able to execute Skype™, also needs to manage the `skype_home_t` files (in case, manual intervention in `~/.Skype/` is needed or to make backups), we grant it both manage privileges as well as relabel privileges. The relabel privileges are needed when, for instance, a backup is restored.

For the user domain, we then call the `skype_role` interface we just created. In the example, we used the `optional_policy` statement. This allows policy modules to be loaded even when one of the calls cannot be resolved or is not supported.

Suppose we need to unload the `myskype` module. Without the `optional_policy` statement, the `myunprivuser` module would need to be unloaded as well, even though this policy module might contain other rules that are important for the user domain to work correctly (in the example, we only called the `skype_role` interface, but after some time, the module might call many other interfaces as well). If we don't unload the module and no `optional_policy` statements are used, then SELinux will warn the administrator about unresolved dependencies between the modules.

With the `optional_policy` statement, the SELinux tools know that the call might become unresolvable, in which case, the entire block (everything inside the `optional_policy` block) will be ignored while the module remains loaded.

There's more...

At the beginning of the recipe, we mentioned that unconfined user domains will be able to execute the application without a domain transition. This is to be expected, as the entire idea behind unconfined domains is that they are, well, unconfined.

It is considered a bad practice to, in general, create domain transitions from an unconfined domain to confined domains. Only in very specific circumstances do domain transitions from an unconfined domain to confined domains make sense (such as when the target domain is used to confine potentially vulnerable applications, such as a sandbox domain).

From a security perspective, it makes more sense to confine users immediately and use the proper domain transitions between (confined) user domains and the application domains.

Testing and enhancing the policy

With the policy ready and loaded, it is time to start testing the application from a user's perspective, while keeping an eye on the audit logs (for denials) and application output.

Testing the application is an important phase of policy development and will also be the most time consuming task. During testing, several functional features of the application will be tried and the resulting permissions (SELinux-wise) will need to be added to the policy.

In previous recipes, such as *Creating a skeleton policy*, we enabled a set of permissions based on other policies and common sense. However, these permissions have not been validated and tested yet. In this recipe, we will assert that the permissions are truly needed, as we do not want to create a policy with too many rights associated with it.

How to do it...

Testing policies is a repetitive task. Every try-out means that the AVC denials leading up to the start need to be discarded (as we do not want to include privileges not related to the test) after which the application is tested and the results are documented. Depending on how the application acts, new policy rules are added to the policy:

1. Write down the current timestamp or create a reference point inside the audit logs (for instance, by reloading the SELinux policy), so we know from which point in the audit logs we need to look at the audit events:

   ```
   ~# semodule -R
   ```

2. As an end user, start the application (from a terminal window) and watch what happens.

3. Write down the error that is displayed (if any):

   ```
   ~$ skype

   skype: error while loading shared libraries: cannot restore
   segment prot after reloc: Permission denied
   ```

4. Look into the denials as displayed in the audit logs:

   ```
   ~# ausearch -m avc -ts recent
   ```

5. For each first denial or denial related to the error shown earlier, try to enhance the policy with the proper call and try again.

How it works...

In this phase, we are enhancing the policy step by step. Some policy developers like to run the application in permissive mode (either by running the entire system in permissive mode or by marking this particular domain as a permissive domain), registering all accesses performed (through the AVC denials) and enhancing the policy based on that information. Although this might give a faster working policy, these developers will also risk that they add too many privileges to a policy, something that is very difficult to challenge and change later.

Instead, we let SELinux prevent accesses and look at how the application reacts. Based on the error logging of the application or the behavior of the application and the AVC denial(s) seen through the logs, we can have a good picture of what privileges are really needed.

For instance, simultaneously with the error presented in the example, the following denial occurred:

```
type=AVC msg=audit(1398930752.113:608): avc: denied { execmod }
for pid=8943 comm="skype" path="/opt/bin/skype" dev="dm-2"
ino=801 scontext=user_u:user_r:skype_t:s0
tcontext=user_u:user_r:skype_exec_t:s0 tclass=file
```

It is important that we focus on the first set of denials that occur and not on all denials shown. It is very likely that denials shown after the first set of denials are from error handling routines, either by the application or the system in general, which would never be triggered in the first place if the proper permissions are granted to the domain. Trying to grant those privileges as well would result in a too broadly defined set of permissions.

The preceding denial shown would result in the following addition to the policy:

```
# Error 'cannot restore segment prot after reloc'
allow skype_t skype_exec_t:file execmod;
```

Ignoring permissions we don't need

After repeated testing, we will have a policy that works, even though denials might still show up in the audit logs. In order not to alarm any administrator, we might want to disable auditing of those specific denials (while, of course, ensuring that critical access vectors are still logged by the audit daemon).

How to do it...

In order to disable logging of certain denials that do not influence an application's behavior, trigger the denial and then register the `dontaudit` statements as explained in the following steps:

1. For each denial shown in the audit logs, we need to find the corresponding `dontaudit` rule set. Consider the following instance:

   ```
   type=AVC msg=audit(1398936489.877:2464): avc: denied {
   search } for pid=8241 comm="skype" name="modules"
   dev="dm-0" ino=1322041 scontext=user_u:user_r:skype_t:s0
   tcontext=user_u:object_r:user_home_t:s0 tclass=dir
   ```

2. Search through the SELinux policies for `dontaudit` statements on this matter:

   ```
   ~$ sefindif dontaudit.*user_home_t.*search

   interface(`userdom_dontaudit_search_user_home_content',`

       dontaudit $1 user_home_t:dir search_dir_perms;
   ```

3. Add in the interface call to the policy, rebuild the policy, and then reload it. Repeat until all cosmetic denials are no longer visible.

How it works...

Many operations performed by applications can be seen as cosmetic—although in the example, the application really performs the searches through the user files, they are not needed for the application to function correctly. For instance, it might be searching through the entire directory until it finds its own files, which it does have access to.

By adding the `dontaudit` statements for these operations, we ensure that the audit logs stay clean.

In case of problems, the administrator can still disable the `dontaudit` statements in the policy, revealing every denial that SELinux has triggered (even those that are explicitly marked as `dontaudit`):

```
~# semodule -DB
```

To re-enable the `dontaudit` statements, rebuild and reload the policy:

```
~# semodule -B
```

In certain situations, there might not be an interface related to `dontaudit` available. In that case, create a new interface (as part of an SELinux policy module) with the `dontaudit` rules defined in it. For instance, for a `dontaudit` rule set to ignore getting the attributes of `mozilla_home_t` content, we would create a `mymozilla` policy module with the `mozilla_dontaudit_getattr_home` interface declared in it.

Creating application resource interfaces

Our application policy is almost ready for deployment. However, it currently is mainly end user focused, and there are no ways of interacting with the `skype_t` domain (or other resources managed by the `skype` module) except through the `skype_role` interface.

In this recipe, we'll add an interface for reading `skype_home_t`.

How to do it...

Alongside the `skype_role` interface that we created in the *Defining application role interfaces* recipe, we need to create additional resource interfaces so that other domains can easily interact with the newly created policy:

1. Open the `myskype.if` file and add in the following content:

    ```
    interface(`skype_read_home',`
      gen_require(`
        type skype_home_t;
      ')
      userdom_search_user_home_dirs($1)
      allow $1 skype_home_t:dir list_dir_perms;
      allow $1 skype_home_t:file read_file_perms;
      allow $1 skype_home_t:lnk_file read_lnk_file_perms;
    ')
    ```

How it works...

The recipe itself is simple—for each interaction with resources managed by the `skype` module, we need to create an interface that can be called by other modules.

Each interface should be complete. For instance, in order to read the `skype_home_t` content, a domain will first need to be able to search through the user's home directory (`user_home_dir_t`, which is not the same as `user_home_t` as the former is the type for the home directory while the latter is for its contents); hence, the call to `userdom_search_user_home_dirs`.

Then, the necessary privileges are assigned to the domain. As we do not provide any class identifier in the interface name, the interface will grant read access to all (significant) classes related to the `skype_home_t` type.

If we only want to grant read access to files (and not to the `directory` class), then the interface would be called `skype_read_home_files`.

Adding conditional policy rules

We can further fine-tune our policy with conditionals. Some of the access vectors identified earlier might not be necessary in all circumstances, so it makes sense to make them optional and configurable through SELinux Booleans.

Two of the identified access vectors that are candidates for configurable policies are as follows:

▸ Accessing the video and sound devices (in order to reduce the risk of malware or vulnerabilities in the application to access the webcam or sound device and spy on the unsuspecting users)

▸ Accessing all user content (instead of only the `skype_home_t` content)

How to do it...

The following set of steps allows us to make the policy more flexible for the administrators to handle by introducing Booleans. These Booleans modify the behavior of the policy and are added to a policy.

1. Inside `myskype.te`, create the definitions for both Booleans. This is usually done before the type declarations:

   ```
   gen_tunable(skype_use_audio, false)
   gen_tunable(skype_use_video, false)
   gen_tunable(skype_manage_user_content, false)
   ```

2. Inside the policy, group the statements that we want to trigger through the Booleans:

   ```
   tunable_policy(`skype_use_audio',`
     dev_read_sound(skype_t)
     dev_write_sound(skype_t)
   ')
   tunable_policy(`skype_use_video',`
     dev_read_video_dev(skype_t)
     dev_write_video_dev(skype_t)
   ')
   tunable_policy(`skype_manage_user_content',`
     userdom_manage_user_home_content_dirs(skype_t)
     userdom_manage_user_home_content_files(skype_t)
   ')
   ```

How it works...

The `gen_tunable` declarations will generate Booleans that administrators can toggle on the system. The first argument of each declaration is the name of the Boolean to be created, while the second argument sets the default value of the Boolean.

Once Booleans are defined, the `tunable_policy` statements allow for grouping the statement calls that need to be made configurable.

It is possible to have rules enabled when a Boolean is disabled as well. For instance, for the `skype_manage_user_content` one, the following code can be used:

```
tunable_policy(`skype_manage_user_content',`
  # boolean enabled
  userdom_manage_user_home_content_dirs(skype_t)
  userdom_manage_user_home_content_files(skype_t)
  ',`
  # boolean disabled
  userdom_dontaudit_manage_user_home_content_dirs(skype_t)
  userdom_dontaudit_read_user_home_content_files(skype_t)
  …
')
```

Booleans can also be combined, as shown in the following code:

```
tunable_policy(`use_nfs_home_dirs && skype_manage_user_content',` … ')
```

In such situations, the policy group rules will only take effect if both the Booleans are enabled.

It is also possible to only enable rules if a Boolean is not set, as shown in the next line of code:

```
tunable_policy(`!use_nfs_home_dirs',` … ')
```

There's more...

Tunable policies are a powerful extension to SELinux. However, there are some caveats to this:

- It is not simple to make the description of SELinux Booleans available to the administrator. The descriptions are defined through in-policy comments, but this is not used for custom modules—a full policy build needs to be made in order to generate the `policy.xml` file that contains all descriptions.

- It is not possible to assign attributes within a `tunable_policy` group. Instead, policy developers will need to make the permissions related to the attribute configurable (if possible) or not assign the attribute at all.

- ▶ It is not possible to use named file transitions within a `tunable_policy` group. In general, that doesn't matter that much—there are a few situations where a named file transition would depend on a Boolean, but these situations do occur.

- ▶ It is not possible to have the `optional_policy` statements within a `tunable_policy` group. Instead, wrap the `tunable_policy` call with an `optional_policy` statement first. It might be needed to create multiple blocks if a single Boolean would trigger multiple policy calls that warrant the use of an `optional_policy` block.

Efforts are being made to remove these shortcomings from the SELinux subsystem though.

Adding build-time policy decisions

The last enhancement we might want to look at is build-time policy decisions. Unlike SELinux Booleans, these are policy blocks that are enabled (or disabled) based on build parameters. We have encountered a few of these in the past already, namely `enable_mcs`, `enable_mls` as well as distribution selection parameters, such as `distro_gentoo` or `distro_redhat`.

In this recipe, we will enable the `xdg_manage_downloads_home` call but only when the policy is built for a Gentoo system.

How to do it...

Build-time decisions are added to the policy using the `ifdef` statements, as can be seen through the next set of steps:

1. Open `myskype.te` and add in the following block of code:

   ```
   ifdef(`distro_gentoo',`
     xdg_manage_downloads_home(skype_t)
   ')
   ```

2. Rebuild the policy. On a Gentoo system, we can confirm that the access is now granted through `sesearch`, whereas other distributions probably don't even know the `xdg_downloads_home_t` type:

   ```
   ~$ sesearch -s skype_t -t xdg_downloads_home_t -A
   ```

How it works...

The reference policy build system automatically defines a couple of parameters that can be used by the `ifdef` macros. The build system uses definitions inside the `build.conf` file available at `/usr/share/selinux/mcs/include/` or `/usr/share/selinux/devel/include/` to generate such parameters.

For instance, the distribution parameter in `build.conf` is set as follows:

```
DISTRO ?= gentoo
```

Inside `Makefile`, this is converted into an `M4PARAM` setting:

```
ifneq ($(DISTRO),)
        M4PARAM += -D distro_$(DISTRO)
endif
```

Through these `M4` parameters, we can then use the `ifdef` statements to query the existence of these parameters and make build-time decisions.

There's more...

It is possible to add our own set of parameters. For this, we set the `M4PARAM` environment variable before we call the `make` command (used while building the policy modules).

For instance, to support the `debug` statements, we could set the following in the policy:

```
ifdef(`debug',` ... ')
```

During policy build, we can enable these statements as follows:

```
~$ export M4PARAM="-D debug"
~$ make mypolicy.pp
```

5

Creating a Server Policy

In this chapter, we will cover the following recipes:

- ► Understanding the service
- ► Choosing resource types wisely
- ► Differentiating policies based on use cases
- ► Creating resource-access interfaces
- ► Creating exec, run, and transition interfaces
- ► Creating a stream-connect interface
- ► Creating the administrative interface

Introduction

Desktop application policies protect a user from vulnerabilities within the application or from unwanted behavior exerted by the application. On a server, however, the impact can be much larger. Server policies are used to protect the entire system from unwanted behavior, abusive access by users, or exploited vulnerabilities within the application.

Services also have a long lifetime. Unlike desktop applications, which usually start up and shut down together with the users' daily work cycle, services tend to run nonstop, 24/7. This not only provides a larger time window to try and exploit these services, but also happens in the background with services that the administrator might not be actively watching.

Understanding the service

The first aspect of designing server policies is to understand the service at hand. Each service has its own internal architecture, and understanding how the various processes and resources interact with each other is extremely important.

Only when the internal architecture is fully understood will we be able to create a properly functioning policy. Otherwise, we risk that the policy will be too broad (too many access rights) or too restricted. Unlike applications, which are usually easy to test from an end user point of view, services often have activities that are much harder to test (or even consider).

How to do it...

Just like with desktop applications, understanding the application behavior is of key importance to create good SELinux policies. Research into and analysis of the behavior can be done by performing the following steps:

1. Research the service at large by looking for online architecture drawings or architecture documentation.

2. Try to explore the service in a sandbox environment.

3. Follow some tutorials for the service with relation to both administration tasks as well as end user tasks.

4. Structurally document how the service should be used.

How it works...

Understanding a service means to get some degree of experience with the administration of the service. Trying to create a server policy for a specific database technology, but not knowing how this database technology works, will be almost impossible.

Online research

Most services have well documented architectural information available online. By using an Internet search engine, we can easily come to the architecture information for a particular service.

While developing service policies, it is considered a best practice that the types and domains are named similar to the functional services that are used. For instance, in a Postfix architecture, functional services such as `pickup`, `cleanup`, `smtpd`, `qmgr`, and many more are basic services that a Postfix administrator has to deal with. In SELinux policies, we should try to have the domains labeled similarly (so the domain will be labeled `postfix_qmgr_t` for the `qmgr` service, `postfix_spool_maildrop_t` for the `maildrop` queue, and so on).

Sandbox environment

Being able to play around with a service in a sandbox environment allows us to see the interactions at hand. It also allows us to follow online tutorials or administration guides to get to know the service.

There are many technologies available nowadays to play around with technologies. Virtualization allows users to run complete systems in an isolated environment and has led to the creation of virtual appliances.

Virtual appliances are virtual images that can be easily installed in a virtualized environment. However, a pure virtualization still requires users to install an operating system, install the service, and configure it before really starting to use it; virtual appliances provide preconfigured systems that host one or more services out of the box.

Next to virtualization, containers are also starting to play a large role. Unlike virtualization, software running inside containers is isolated from other software but is still part of the operating system itself.

The structural documentation

After having a thorough read through the architecture of the application and perhaps even playing around with the software, we might need to document the architecture of the service further in order to deduce the right SELinux types and resources, as well as interfaces and roles related to the service.

In order not to forget anything important, the logical architecture of a service can be documented using the **FAMOUS** abbreviation:

- **Feeds**: This tells us which external resources provide input to the service in a more-or-less batch-oriented approach as well as which external resources the service interacts with.

- **Administration**: This informs us how the service is administered (command-line interfaces, user interfaces, or other applications).

- **Monitoring**: This informs us about logfiles used or commands that are supported to verify the state of the service.

- **Operations**: This documents the day-to-day runtime behavior of all the processes (and the flows, using the CRUD method—Create, Read, Update, Delete). This is usually the architecture information found earlier during the online research phase.

- **Users and rights**: This documents how users are defined and managed in the service. This also documents which authentication or authorization backends are used, how different roles within the service behave, and so forth.

- **Security-related features**: These tell us about security-related features such as application-based access controls, firewall requirements (which in our case are important for the policy network rules), and so forth.

With this information at hand, we can have a clear overview of how the service behaves. For instance, a high-level view of the PostgreSQL database service looks like the following diagram:

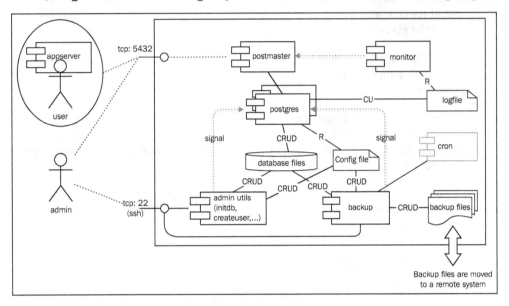

Such a drawing helps us to identify types later on, both for the processes as well as the resources involved. Any interactions with the service provided by third-party services is shown as well, as these interactions will result in privileges that need to be assigned to the other processes (that is, interfaces in the SELinux policy).

It is not easy to document how a service works without understanding the service at hand. Because of the complexity of the service, it is a good practice to get experts or developers of the service together and guide us in understanding the service. These developers and engineers can later be used to challenge the SELinux policy that is being written.

See also

A nonexhaustive list of open source virtual appliance providers is as follows:

- Artica (http://www.artica.fr) for proxy, mail, and NAS appliances.
- Turnkey Linux (http://www.turnkeylinux.org/) offers more than a hundred ready-to-use solutions.
- Vagrant (http://www.vagrantup.com/) is a management platform for virtual systems, and has a large community of Vagrant boxes that provide virtual appliance-like setups for many free software services.
- Docker (https://www.docker.io/) is not a true virtualization setup, but rather a container-based approach. From the Docker Index (https://index.docker.io/), many containers can be freely downloaded.

Many commercial technologies also provide development virtual machines to deploy. Virtualization technology providers such as VMware® have solution-exchange communities, where virtual images for various technologies are freely available.

Choosing resource types wisely

Services interact with resources, and the label that we assign to the resources is used by the fine-grained access controls assigned to these resources. End user files (for users that have a Linux account on the system) are labeled as `user_home_t`, which suffices for most uses. However, when we deal with services, the choice of the resource label defines if and how other applications can access those resources and is much more fine-grained than what we currently use for end user files.

There are some best practices concerning resource type selection within SELinux policies, which we will now look into.

How to do it...

The service resource types need to be carefully chosen. Their naming implies the functional use of the resource, which already pushes the development of the policy in a certain structure. The types and their affiliated permissions can be developed by completing the following steps:

1. Look for the processes that will run within their own specific domain and create the domain types. For each domain, look for the entry files of that domain and create an `_exec_t` type. Mark the type as either an init daemon type (when the service is launched through a service script) or a D-Bus daemon (when the service is launched through the D-Bus service). For instance, for the BIND service:

   ```
   type named_t;
   type named_exec_t;
   init_daemon_domain(named_t, named_exec_t)
   ```

2. Look for all sets of logical resources that are used by the application. These are often files specific to the service architecture (such as database files for a database service), but shouldn't be limited to files only.

3. Create specific types for these resources. For instance, for the Qemu virtual guest images:

   ```
   type qemu_image_t;
   files_type(qemu_image_t)
   ```

4. Grant the domains the proper access to these resources. For instance, the qemu process (running as `qemu_t`) will need manage rights on the images:

   ```
   manage_files_pattern(qemu_t, qemu_image_t, qemu_image_t)
   ```

5. Go through the infrastructural resources (PID files, logfiles, and configuration files) and label these accordingly. For instance, for the `named` variable, the runtime data will be named as follows:

```
type named_var_run_t;
files_pid_file(named_var_run_t)
```

6. Grant the domains the proper access to these resources, and if possible, enable a proper file transition:

```
allow named_t named_var_run_t:file manage_files_perms;
allow named_t named_var_run_t:sock_file
  manage_sock_file_perms;
files_pid_filetrans(named_t, named_var_run_t, { file
  sock_file });
```

How it works...

An application policy always provides a common set of privileges. It starts with proper domain definitions (showing how the policy will be structured) and is followed by the resource access patterns. Resources can be functional in nature (specific to the application that is being investigated for the policy) or more infrastructural (such as logfiles and configuration files).

Domain definitions

Service domains are used to identify long-running processes that have a similar functional scope. An example could be the BIND named process (which is defined as `named_t`) or the Apache `httpd` processes (which are all running as `httpd_t`).

These service domains are usually launched from an `init` script, which results in the use of the `init_daemon_domain` interface. If a service is launched by D-Bus, then the interface to use is `dbus_system_domain`. Of course, multiple interfaces can be used: the PPP daemon, for instance, supports both `init` scripts and D-Bus.

If a service daemon is launched by another daemon instead, then it is sufficient to mark the process domain as a domain type and the executable type as the entry point:

```
type postfix_bounce_t;
type postfix_bounce_exec_t;
domain_type(postfix_bounce_t)
domain_entry_file(postfix_bounce_t, postfix_bounce_exec_t)
```

In this case, we need to provide the parent domain (in our case, `postfix_master_t`) the rights to execute (`postfix_bounce_exec_t`) and transition (to `postfix_bounce_t`):

```
domtrans_pattern(postfix_master_t, postfix_bounce_exec_t,
postfix_bounce_t)
```

Logical resources

The logical resources are the files that are specific to the applications' functional design. For instance, a virtualization layer such as Qemu will have a logical resource for the image files (`qemu_image_t`). The logical resources for a web server have already been discussed in an earlier chapter (such as `httpd_sys_content_t` for standard system read-only web content).

Such resources are declared as regular file resources and the proper permissions are granted to the various domains. Further down the document, when privileges for the `qemu_t` domain are summed up, the `manage_files_pattern` line can be added to allow the `qemu_t` domain to manage the images.

By making separate labels for each of the logical resources, we can create interfaces for other processes that might need to interact with these resources without having to grant those applications too many privileges.

Think of a backup application, such as Amanda. The actual backup data itself (`amanda_data_t`) should only be accessible by the Amanda application. Other service administrators on the same system should not have access to these files—backups can contain sensitive information, so only the backup tool itself should have access to this data. Even the backup administrators, who need to manage the backup infrastructure, might not need direct access to this data.

Infrastructural resources

Infrastructural resources are file types that are often set for applications.

Logfiles are marked through the `logging_log_file` interface and usually end with the `_log_t` suffix, such as `amanda_log_t`. By marking it as a logfile, domains that are assigned an operation concerning all logfiles (such as `logging_read_all_logs`) automatically have these privileges on the newly defined type. Often, a file transition is set so that files created in `/var/log/` automatically get the right type. This is done through the `logging_log_filetrans` interface:

```
type amanda_log_t;
logging_log_file(amanda_log_t)
# Directories created by amanda_t domain in /var/log (var_log_t) get
the amanda_log_t type:
logging_log_filetrans(amanda_t, amanda_log_t, dir)
```

Configuration files are marked as regular files (through `files_type`) and end with either `_conf_t` or `_etc_t`. Some policy developers like to use `_conf_t` for real configuration files and `_etc_t` for other miscellaneous files in the `/etc/` directory structure that are not direct configuration files. In most cases though, this is only for semantic reasons as all related domains need the same set of privileges on both types.

Temporary files are marked through the `files_tmp_file` interface and end with the `_tmp_t` suffix. A file transition is almost always put in place to ensure that the temporary files are properly labeled:

```
type amanda_tmp_t;
files_tmp_file(amanda_tmp_t)
# All files, directories and symbolic links created by amanda_t in
a tmp_t location should get the amanda_tmp_t label:
files_tmp_filetrans(amanda_t, amanda_tmp_t, { dir lnk_file file })
```

PID files and other generic run files are usually labeled ending with `_var_run_t` and are marked as a PID file through the `files_pid_file` interface. As with logfiles, a file transition is usually put in place as well:

```
type amanda_var_run_t;
files_pid_file(amanda_var_run_t)
# Files and sockets created in /var/run should become
amanda_var_run_t:
files_pid_filetrans(amanda_t, amanda_var_run_t,
{ file sock_file })
```

Other variable data that is not given a logical resource name is often labeled ending with `_var_lib_t`. Such files are marked as regular files (using `file_type`) and a file transition can be defined using `files_var_lib_filetrans`.

Differentiating policies based on use cases

As services mature, they often gain more features, which might not always be necessary. For instance, daemons that are able to optionally connect to various network resources depending on their configuration should not be allowed by the SELinux policy to always connect to various network resources.

To govern these features, SELinux policy developers include Booleans to selectively toggle policies based on the administrator's requirements.

How to do it...

Booleans allow policy developers to create policy rules that only participate in access control when the administrator has elected to use them. For services in particular, this is often used to optionally allow privileges based on the use case of the service and is implemented as follows:

1. Identify the policy blocks that should be marked as optional, depending on the configuration. For instance, this could be a set of policy rules that allow PostgreSQL to connect to other PostgreSQL databases:

```
corenet_tcp_connect_postgresql_port(postgresql_t)
corenet_sendrecv_postgresql_client_packets(postgresql_t)
```

2. For each block, create a well-chosen SELinux Boolean that administrators can easily identify as the right Boolean to toggle for their specific use case. For instance, we can create a `postgresql_connect_db` Boolean:

```
## <desc>
##    <p>
##       Determine if the PostgreSQL daemons can connect to
other databases.
##    </p>
## </desc>
gen_tunable(postgresql_connect_db, false)
```

3. Surround the policy blocks that need to be toggled with a `tunable_policy` statement for the chosen SELinux Boolean, as follows:

```
tunable_policy(`postgresql_connect_db',`
  corenet_tcp_connect_postgresql_port(postgresql_t)
  corenet_sendrecv_postgresql_client_packets(postgresql_t)
')
```

How it works...

Although we shouldn't over-tune policies by generating dozens of Booleans, isolating functionality that is often abused in exploits is a good practice.

Consider a database engine. Databases can have features that allow them to connect to other databases (for instance, to set up database links or support some kind of cluster), but in many situations, these features are not needed. If a database is compromised (through SQL injection, for instance), it is better to make sure that this database cannot access other databases (so the compromised database is sufficiently contained).

The configuration that toggles this behavior in a PostgreSQL setup could be named `postgresql_connect_db` (for database-specific connections) or `postgresql_connect_all_ports` (for any target connection) and developed as shown in the previous example (the example includes the in-line comment documentation that would be used if the policy is meant to become part of the distribution policy or reference policy project).

Accessing other resources on the network is a common feature that, if it is not part of the standard behavior of the application, should be considered for making optional.

There are many other use cases that should be considered. Here is a nonexhaustive list:

- ▶ An application that can optionally execute system scripts or user-provided scripts should be governed through an `_exec_scripts` or `_exec_user_scripts` Boolean.

- ▶ Allowed domain transitions to higher-privileged domains or increased privileges due to some functionality is usually governed through `_use_*` Booleans. For instance, a domain optionally supporting Java can have a `_use_java` Boolean.

- ▶ Access to specific filesystems or devices is also governed through `_use_*` Booleans, such as `_use_cifs` (for SMB-CIFS filesystems) or `_use_nfs`.

- ▶ Functional support (such as Nginx support for various protocols) can be made optional through `_enable_*` Booleans, such as `nginx_enable_imap_server` or `nginx_enable_pop3_server`.

Creating resource-access interfaces

With all the resources defined, we now need to ensure that other domains can use those resources as needed. As we've seen, resources can be functional in nature (specific to a service) or more infrastructural (such as logfiles).

Access to resources is provided through SELinux policy rules that need to be provided through access interfaces. These interfaces are then used by third-party SELinux policy modules to document and allow access to the resource types. Without the access interfaces, the resource types we define are not easily accessible by other policy developers.

How to do it...

To create resource-access interfaces, add the proper interface definition in the module's `.if` file. For instance, to create a set of resource interfaces to access ClamAV's configuration files, follow the next set of steps:

1. For each resource, create an overview of the privileges that will be needed. For file class resources, these are often search, read, write, and manage privileges. In case of logfiles, some applications only need append privileges (which ensures that they cannot modify existing data, only add data to it).

2. Create the interface in the module's `.if` file and ensure that it is properly documented, as shown in the following code:

```
#############################################
## <summary>
##   Read clamav configuration files
## </summary>
## <param name="domain">
##   <summary>
##   Domain allowed access
```

```
##     </summary>
## </param>
#
interface(`clamav_read_config','
  gen_require(`
    type clamd_etc_t;
  ')
  files_search_etc($1)
  allow $1 clamd_etc_t:file read_file_perms;
')
```

3. Consider creating a `dontaudit` interface as well to assign to SELinux domains that might attempt to perform this action while not needing the privilege:

```
#########################################
## <summary>
##    Do not audit attempts to read the clamd configuration files
## </summary>
## <param name="domain">
##    <summary>
##    Domain not to audit
##    </summary>
## </param>
#
interface(`clamav_dontaudit_read_config',`
  gen_require(`
    type clamd_etc_t;
  ')
  dontaudit $1 clamd_etc_t:file read;
')
```

How it works...

The resource-access interfaces are needed to allow interaction with the SELinux types managed through the SELinux module. The build environment does not have a default set of privilege interfaces that are generated out of the box, so we need to create these interfaces ourselves.

One might be tempted to only create the resource interfaces that are known to be used in the immediate future. However, it is recommended to create the proper interfaces for all resources and each individually with a coherent set of supported privileges. This is because we never know how the resources will be used by others, and by not creating the proper resources, we are forcing other developers to create their own `my*` modules to provide interfaces.

By covering most access patterns towards the resources, we provide a nice set of interfaces that other developers can use while keeping the interfaces all bound to a single module.

Even the `dontaudit` related interfaces will play an important role for the users of the SELinux policy. When policy developers commit policy improvements to repositories, they usually do not `dontaudit` unless they are 100 percent convinced that these will hide cosmetic denials and thus can be ignored. As a result, default SELinux system deployments will have quite a few denials in the audit logs that need to be looked into by the system administrator.

If the administrator doesn't believe that the denials need to be enabled, then they will need to be able to `dontaudit` them. Although the administrator can create the proper interfaces themselves, it is much easier if the `dontaudit` interface definitions are already provided.

Creating exec, run, and transition interfaces

Service domains usually have a few binaries that are executed by user domains or through other service or application domains. Each case of these executions need to be properly investigated to see if a domain transition is needed (that is, a specific domain needs to be created for that execution environment) or if the command can run within the privileges of the caller domain.

From an interface point of view, this is provided through the _exec, _run, and _domtrans interfaces.

How to do it...

Execution-related interfaces allow for other policy modules to define the interaction with this application. This interaction can be a regular execution, but can also contain a domain transition to switch the application domain to the newly defined one. The set of execution interfaces are created as follows:

1. For each execution where the application itself needs to run in the caller domain (so no transition has to occur), create an _exec interface as follows:

```
######################################
## <summary>
##      Execute wm in the caller domain
## </summary>
## <param name="domain">
##      <summary>
##      Domain allowed access
##      </summary>
## </param>
#
interface(`wm_exec',`
   gen_require(`
```

```
    type wm_exec_t;
  ')
  corecmd_search_bin($1)
  can_exec($1, wm_exec_t)
')
```

2. For each execution by a domain that is in the same role as the service (usually, `system_r`) and where a transition has to occur, create a `_domtrans` interface as follows:

```
###########################################
## <summary>
##     Execute vlock in the vlock domain
## </summary>
## <param name="domain">
##     <summary>
##     Domain allowed to transition
##     </summary>
## </param>
#
interface(`vlock_domtrans',`
  gen_require(`
    type vlock_t, vlock_exec_t;
  ')
  corecmd_search_bin($1)
  domtrans_pattern($1, vlock_exec_t, vlock_t)
')
```

3. For each execution by a domain that might not have standard access to the application domain, and where a domain transition has to occur, create a `_run` interface as follows:

```
###########################################
## <summary>
##     Execute vlock in the vlock domain and allow the specific role
the vlock domain
## </summary>
## <param name="domain">
##     <summary>
##     Domain allowed to transition
##     </summary>
## </param>
## <param name="role">
##     <summary>
```

```
##    Role allowed to access the vlock domain
##    </summary>
## </param>
#
interface(`vlock_run',`
  gen_require(`
    attribute_role vlock_roles;
  ')
  vlock_domtrans($1)
  roleattribute $2 vlock_roles;
')
```

How it works...

The use of _exec, _run, and _domtrans are standard interface patterns in policy development. The _role interface that we created during desktop application policy development not only includes domain transition and role support, but also resource accesses related to the user domain interacting with the desktop application domain.

In the _run interface, the only set of privileges that is provided is to transition to the right domain and assign the domain to the right role (as part of SELinux role-based access control). It is common practice that the order of the parameters of a _run interface are the domain first and then the role—unlike the _role interfaces, where the role comes first and then the domain.

In a _domtrans interface, only the domain transition is enabled. Usually, the _run interfaces call the _domtrans interface so that both interfaces are defined and the right one for the job is called by the caller SELinux policy module. But unlike the _run interfaces, the _domtrans interfaces do not extend roles and are usually called by other modules for service domain interaction.

For instance, the procmail_t domain (for the procmail daemon) might call the clamscan application (part of the ClamAV setup) needing to transition to clamscan_t. It does so through the clamav_domtrans_clamscan interface:

```
optional_policy(`
  clamav_domtrans_clamscan(procmail_t)
')
```

Finally, the _exec interface allows a domain to execute a binary without any transition. This interface is needed when a binary is labeled as a specific executable type (not bin_t or shell_exec_t) as most domains then do not have the privilege to access this file at all, let alone execute it. For instance, the Postfix local daemon might call the clamscan executable but does not need to transition, resulting in the following call:

```
optional_policy(`
  clamav_exec_clamscan(procmail_local_t)
')
```

See also

▶ Assigning the newly created interfaces to roles is covered in _Chapter 6, Setting Up Separate Roles_

Creating a stream-connect interface

Be it through the specific executable types or by the generic `bin_t` labeled commands, executions that remain in the caller domain might still require additional privileges to be assigned to the caller domain. These additional privileges could be reading of configuration files or interacting with the main domain through Unix domain sockets or TCP/UDP sockets.

In this recipe, we'll set up a stream-connect interface (as the other privilege enhancements are already covered through the regular resource-access interfaces or network-access interfaces).

How to do it...

Interaction with an application socket can be done either through a socket file or through a named Unix domain socket. This is application-specific, so consulting the application documentation might be necessary up front.

For a Unix domain socket with a socket file

If the stream connection is through a Unix domain socket with a socket file, the interaction with an application socket can be done by completing the following steps:

1. Identify and register the proper types in the `.te` file. Socket files usually have the `_var_run_t` suffix as they reside in `/var/run/`.

2. Create a stream-connect interface that calls `stream_connect_pattern` as follows:

```
interface(`ldap_stream_connect',`
  gen_require(`
    type slapd_t, slapd_var_run_t;
  ')
  files_search_pids($1)
  stream_connect_pattern($1, slapd_var_run_t, slapd_var_run_t,
slapd_t)
')
```

For an abstract Unix domain socket

If the stream connection is through an abstract Unix domain socket (so no socket files are involved), create a stream-connect interface that only provides the `connectto` privilege, as follows:

```
interface(`init_stream_connect',`
  gen_require(`
    type init_t;
  ')
  allow $1 init_t:unix_stream_connect connectto;
')
```

How it works...

Daemons often provide methods to interact with them. Many services support Unix domain socket-based communication between a client application (which usually runs within the privileges of the caller domain) and the daemon itself.

In such cases, the daemon itself creates a socket file (usually in `/var/run/`) as some sort of access point (applications can also use abstract namespaces, where no socket file is needed anymore) and the caller domain is allowed to write to this socket and through it connect to the Unix domain socket held by the daemon. The set of privileges is provided by the `stream_connect_pattern` definition and can be visually represented as follows:

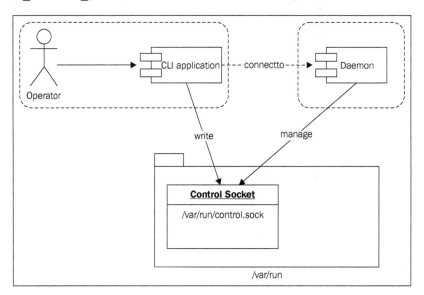

The most important privilege here is the `connectto` privilege between the caller domain and the daemon domain. In case of abstract Unix domain sockets, no socket file is used at all and only the `connectto` privilege is needed.

These privileges are then written in the following domain-specific interface that calls the `stream_connect_pattern` definition, which provides the proper privileges in one go:

```
~$ seshowdef stream_connect_pattern
define(`stream_connect_pattern',`
  allow $1 $2:dir search_dir_perms;
  allow $1 $3:sock_file write_sock_file_perms;
  allow $1 $4:unix_stream_socket connectto;
')
```

If stream-connection-oriented applications are used whose binaries are not labeled as `bin_t`, then a `_stream_connect` interface call is usually seen together with an `_exec` interface call.

Creating the administrative interface

To end the SELinux module development for services, we need to create proper role-based interfaces. Whereas the `_role` interface is usually for nonprivileged user roles, an `_admin` interface is used to provide all the necessary privileges to fully administer a service.

How to do it...

An administrative interface which we can later assign to the user and role that will administer the environment is created with the following steps:

1. Create a specific `init` script type for the `init` scripts of the daemon. For instance, for the `virtd` daemon inside `virt.te`, the following policy rules create the proper `init` script type:

    ```
    type virtd_initrc_exec_t;
    init_script_file(virtd_initrc_exec_t)
    ```

2. Make sure that this `init` script is labeled correctly through the `.fc` file:

    ```
    /etc/rc\.d/init\.d/libvirtd    --
    gen_context(system_u:object_r:virtd_initrc_exec_t,s0)
    ```

3. Start with a skeleton `_admin` interface:

    ```
    ########################################
    ## <summary>
    ##   All rules related to administer a virt environment
    ## </summary>
    ## <param name="domain">
    ##   <summary>
    ##   Domain allowed access
    ##   </summary>
    ## </param>
    ```

```
## <param name="role">
##    <summary>
##    Role allowed access
##    </summary>
## </param>
#
interface(`virt_admin',`
  gen_require(`
    ...
')
```

4. Identify all the resources that an administrator would need access to. Keep in mind that administrators might need to directly modify files that are otherwise managed through the service-related commands—do not take away this right from administrators. A common pattern to use here is `admin_pattern`. Add in the proper rights in the interface (and do not forget to update the `gen_require` block at the beginning). Consider the following example:

    ```
    files_search_tmp($1)
    admin_pattern($1, virt_tmp_t)
    ```

5. Look through the administration guides for other operations that administrators might need with regards to processes. Perhaps there are certain signals that could be allowed to be sent to the daemons:

    ```
    # Allow the admin to run strace or other tracing tools
    against the daemons
    allow $1 virtd_t:process { ptrace signal_perms };
    # Allow admins to view all information related to the
    processes
    ps_process_pattern($1, virtd_t)
    ```

6. Allow the administrator to run the `init` script(s):

    ```
    init_labeled_script_domtrans($1, virtd_initrc_exec_t)
    domain_system_change_exemption($1)
    role_transition $2 virtd_initrc_exec_t system_r;
    allow $2 system_r;
    ```

How it works...

The `_admin` interface is meant to contain all the privileges needed for an (otherwise) unprivileged user to administer a service. In essence, this unprivileged user will become privileged for this particular service, gaining just those rights that the user needs in order to manage the service, but nothing more.

We start by defining a particular `init` script type for the service. By default, the `init` scripts are labeled `initrc_exec_t` and only the system administrator is allowed to execute them. As we do not want to give a specific service administrator the privileges to execute any `init` script, we create a specific script type (`_initrc_exec_t`) and then allow the user, through the `_admin` interface, to execute that particular script type.

The latter, however, is more than just creating execute rights (which is done through the `init_labeled_script_domtrans` call). Executing the script also means that the script itself has to run in the `system_r` role. If we do not enforce this, then the script would (attempt to) run in the role of the caller domain (such as `virtadm_r`) and fail, as the `initrc_t` domain (the type used for the `init` scripts) is not allowed for the `virtadm_r` role.

Transitioning a role upon executing a file is done through the `role_transition` directive. In our example, we configure that the user role (such as `virtadm_r`) transitions to the `system_r` role upon executing `virtd_initrc_exec_t`:

```
role_transition $2 virtd_initrc_exec_t system_r;
```

We need to allow the `system_r` role for the given user role as well, which is done through the `allow $2 system_r` call. But even that is not sufficient.

SELinux has a constraint in place that prevents transitions to `system_r`, as the `system_r` role is used for all system services and, as such, is a highly privileged role. The constraint is defined so that only specific domains can trigger a transition to `system_r`. With the `domain_system_change_exemption` call, we mark the user domain as one of these domains.

Besides the `init` script-related permissions, most `_admin` interfaces provide administrative rights to almost all resources provided by the module. To simplify policy development, the `admin_pattern` call is used. This pattern not only provides manage rights (read, write, execute, delete, and so on) on the resources, but also relabel rights, allowing the administrator to relabel files and directories as the resource types used in the module (or vice versa, relabel from those types to other types the administrator has relabel privileges to).

With these relabel rights, administrators can call `restorecon` against files to label them correctly (if properly defined in the SELinux policy) or use `chcon` to specifically set a label.

See also

▸ Creating new administrative roles is covered in *Chapter 6, Setting Up Separate Roles*

115

6
Setting Up
Separate Roles

In this chapter, we will cover the following topics:

- ▶ Managing SELinux users
- ▶ Mapping Linux users to SELinux users
- ▶ Running commands in a specified role with sudo
- ▶ Running commands in a specified role with runcon
- ▶ Switching roles
- ▶ Creating a new role
- ▶ Initial role based on entry
- ▶ Defining role transitions
- ▶ Looking into access privileges

Introduction

Roles provide a flexible, manageable approach to grant multiple users the proper rights. Instead of assigning privileges to individual users, roles are created to which privileges are granted. Users are then granted the role and inherit the privileges associated with this role.

In SELinux, roles are used to grant access to domains. An application domain that is used to manage certificates on a system is assigned to one or more roles, thus allowing users with that role to possibly transition into that application domain. If the user role does not have this privilege, then the necessary permissions to manage certificates through that application domain are not accessible for the user.

The following diagram shows the relation between Linux logins (regular Linux accounts), SELinux users, SELinux roles, and SELinux domains:

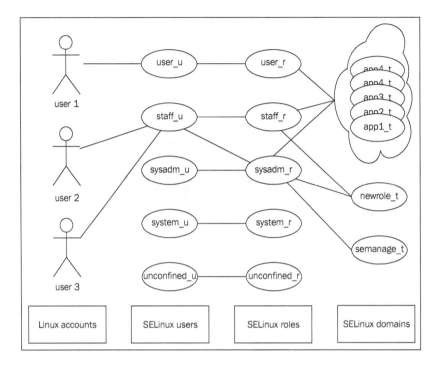

To assign roles to users, Linux accounts are first mapped to an SELinux user. An SELinux user defines which roles are accessible (as users can have multiple roles assigned) as well as which security clearance the user can have at most (although lower security clearances can be assigned to users individually as well).

On systems where SELinux is primarily meant to confine network-facing services and not the users, this chapter will have little value. All users on these systems are mapped to the `unconfined_u` SELinux user, which has a default user domain of `unconfined_t` and is meant to be almost unrestricted—hence, the name, unconfined. When this is applicable, most distributions call the SELinux policy store **targeted** to reflect that the confinement is targeting specific applications and not the entire system.

Managing SELinux users

In order to grant a Linux login the right set of roles, we first need to create an SELinux user that has just those roles assigned. Existing SELinux users can be modified easily, and if an SELinux user was added previously, it can be removed from the system as well.

How to do it...

Managing SELinux users is done as follows:

1. Use `semanage user` to list the currently available SELinux users:

```
~# semanage user -l

                      Labeling    MLS/        MLS/
SELinux User          Prefix      MCS Level   MCS Range
SELinux Roles


git_shell_u           user        s0          s0
git_shell_r
guest_u               user        s0          s0
guest_r
root                  user        s0          s0-s0:c0.c1023
staff_r sysadm_r system_r unconfined_r
staff_u               user        s0          s0-s0:c0.c1023
staff_r sysadm_r system_r unconfined_r
sysadm_u              user        s0          s0-s0:c0.c1023
sysadm_r
system_u              user        s0          s0-s0:c0.c1023
system_r unconfined_r
unconfined_u          user        s0          s0-s0:c0.c1023
system_r unconfined_r
user_u                user        s0          s0
user_r
xguest_u              user        s0          s0
xguest_r
```

2. If no SELinux user exists yet, with the right set of roles, create it with `semanage user`. For instance, to create a database administration SELinux user, run the following command:

```
~# semanage user -a -R "staff_r dbadm_r" dbadm_u
```

3. Existing users can be modified as follows:

```
~# semanage user -m -R "staff_r dbadm_r" staff_u
```

4. An SELinux user can also be removed from the system:

```
~# semanage user -d dbadm_u
```

How it works...

When an SELinux user is created, SELinux will update its configuration files at `/etc/selinux/` to include support for this SELinux user. It is a general best practice to name SELinux users after their functional purpose, so a **database administrator** (**DBA**) is called `dbadm_u`, whereas a website administrator is called `webadm_u`.

The set of roles that are available to the administrator can be obtained using `seinfo`:

```
~# seinfo -r
```

Existing SELinux users can be modified. However, it is important that logged-in users are logged out (and perhaps temporarily locked) from the system during the change. Otherwise, the SELinux policy could suddenly mark their session as having an invalid context and interrupt those users in their operations.

When an SELinux user is removed from the system, it is also important that all the remaining files that have this SELinux user in their context are relabeled. Otherwise, these files (and other resources) are labeled with an invalid context, making the files and resources inaccessible to others.

Once an SELinux user is created, it is ready to be assigned to one or more Linux users.

There's more...

With SELinux users, MLS settings can be provided as well. For instance, to set a specific security clearance, the following command is used:

```
~# semanage user -a -r s0-s0:c0.c110 dbadm_u
```

For an SELinux user, this is the upper limit of the security clearance that a users' context can be in. When we assign users to an SELinux user, it is possible to force a lower security clearance individually so that there is no need to create separate SELinux users for every difference in security clearance.

Mapping Linux users to SELinux users

With the SELinux users available, we can now map Linux users to SELinux users. This will ensure that the users, when logged in to the system, are assigned a default context aligned with this SELinux user.

How to do it...

In order to map Linux users to SELinux users, the following steps can be taken:

1. List the existing mappings with `semanage login`:

   ```
   ~# semanage login -l
   Login Name              SELinux User              MLS/MCS Range

   __default__             user_u                    s0-s0:c0.c1023
   root                    root                      s0-s0:c0.c1023
   system_u                system_u                  s0-s0:c0.c1023
   %wheel                  sysadm_u                  s0-s0:c0.c1023
   ```

2. For an individual user account, map the account to an SELinux user with `semanage login`:

   ```
   ~# semanage login -a -s dbadm_u user1
   ```

3. It is also possible to assign a group of users to an SELinux user through their primary Linux group. For instance, if a `dba` group exists, it can be assigned to an SELinux user as follows:

   ```
   ~# semanage login -a -s dbadm_u %dba
   ```

4. Mappings can be modified easily:

   ```
   ~# semanage login -m -s webadm_u user1
   ```

5. If a mapping is no longer needed, it can be removed as well:

   ```
   ~# semanage login -d user1
   ```

How it works...

The `semanage login` application manages the `seusers` file in `/etc/selinux/`. This file is used by SELinux's `pam_selinux.so` authentication library that is called when a user logs in to a system. Upon invocation, SELinux will check the `seusers` file to see which SELinux user a Linux account is mapped to. It will then perform an SELinux context switch so that the rest of the login process (including the shell or graphical environment that is launched) will have the right SELinux context assigned to it.

Creating login mappings does not influence the existing sessions, so if a user is already logged in, it is wise to have the user log out first. Also, any files created by the user in the past might have a wrong SELinux user associated with them. Any login that isn't specifically mentioned will be assigned a default SELinux user. If the SELinux user changes, then the files owned by this Linux login will suddenly have a wrong SELinux user set. If the user-based access control feature in SELinux is enabled, then these files will not be accessible anymore by the user. In this case, the administrator will need to relabel the files forcefully (which includes resetting the SELinux user):

```
~# restorecon -RF /home/user1
```

In case of both user mappings and group-based mappings, the first mapping that is mentioned in the `seusers` file that matches a particular login is used.

When a user logs in and no mapping matches the login itself (either through a direct match against a Linux account name or through a group membership), then SELinux will look at the login mapping for the `__default__` user. This is a special rule that acts as a fallback rule. On systems with unconfined users, the `__default__` user is usually mapped to the `unconfined_u` SELinux user. On systems without unconfined users, `__default__` usually maps to the (unprivileged) `user_u` SELinux user.

Running commands in a specified role with sudo

When a user has been assigned multiple roles, they usually work with their primary role (such as `staff_r`) and only selectively execute commands with the other role. This can be accomplished through the `sudo` command, as these commands usually also require a different Linux user (which can be `root` or the `postgresql` account for DBA tasks on the PostgreSQL database server).

How to do it...

In order to configure `sudo` to perform the right role and type transition, execute the following steps:

1. Open up the `sudoers` file through `visudo`:

   ```
   ~# visudo
   ```

2. Define the commands that the user(s) are allowed to execute. For instance, to allow all users in the `dba` group to call `initdb` in the `dbadm_r` role, define the commands as follows:

   ```
   %dba ALL=(postgres) ROLE="dbadm_r" TYPE="dbadm_t" /usr/sbin/initdb
   ```

3. The users in the `dba` group can now call `initdb`, and `sudo` will automatically switch to the `dbadm_r` role and the `dbadm_t` user domain when `initdb` is called:

```
~$ sudo -u postgres initdb
```

How it works...

The regular user domains that users run with are, by default, not that privileged. Although it is possible to extend the privileges of the role and user domains directly, the best segregation is provided through different roles. Such an approach allows unprivileged user domains, such as `staff_t`, to be used by multiple, different organizational roles (and thus, SELinux users).

Once a privileged command needs to be executed, users will need to switch their active role. If this is only needed for a small set of commands, which also require switching the Linux user itself (such as switching to the `postgres` runtime account), then privilege delegation tools such as `sudo` are often used.

The `sudo` command is an SELinux-aware application that can be configured to assist in switching the SELinux context as well. This can be done through the command line directly if the user wants:

```
~$ sudo -u postgres -r dbadm_r -t dbadm_t initdb
```

However, most administrators will want to configure this in the `sudoers` file. This is more user friendly as the end user does not need to continuously pass the role and type parts of the context in which commands need to be executed.

Of course, this requires that the SELinux user that is calling `sudo` has the privilege to run commands in the `dbadm_r` role. If not, then even if the `sudoers` file mentions that the user can execute the command, the transition (and thus, the command) will fail, as shown in the following command:

```
~$ sudo -u postgres initdb
sudo: webadm_u:dbadm_r:dbadm_t:s0-s0:c0.c1023 is not a valid context
```

See also

For more information on `sudo` and the `sudoers` file, check out their associated manual pages:

```
~$ man sudo
```
```
~$ man sudoers
```

The main project site for the `sudo` application is at `https://www.sudo.ws`.

Running commands in a specified role with runcon

Using `sudo` is not mandatory. SELinux also provides a command called `runcon` that allows users to run a command in a different context. Of course, SELinux restrictions still apply—the user must have the proper privileges to execute commands with a different context.

How to do it...

Running a command using a specified role and type is done by completing the following steps:

1. Identify the domain in which the command should run, usually by checking the executables' context and searching for the `entrypoint` definition:

   ```
   ~$ ls -Z auditctl
   system_u:object_r:auditctl_exec_t    auditctl
   ~$ sesearch -t auditctl_exec_t -c file -p entrypoint -A
   Found 1 semantic av rules:
       allow auditctl_t auditctl_exec_t : file { … entrypoint … };
   ```

2. Call the command, passing along the role and target type:

   ```
   ~$ runcon -r secadm_r -t auditctl_t auditctl -l
   ```

How it works...

The `runcon` application tells SELinux that the invocation of the command should result in a type and role transition towards the specified type (`auditctl_t`) and role (`secadm_r`). SELinux will perform multiple checks and validations before this will actually succeed. These checks are as follows:

▶ Does the current user have the right to execute `auditctl` (execute rights on `auditctl_exec_t`)?

▶ Is a role switch from the current role (say `staff_r`) to the new role (`secadm_r`) allowed?

▶ Is there a policy in place that allows transition from the current type (say `staff_t`) to the selected type (`auditctl_t`)?

▶ Is `auditctl_t` a valid target domain if the executed file is `auditctl_exec_t` (which is the `entrypoint` check)?

▶ Is the target context (such as `staff_u:secadm_r:auditctl_t`) a valid context (which implies that the current SELinux user has access to the given role)?

The `runcon` application can be used when no Linux user transition needs to occur (although this doesn't exclude the use of `sudo`). In the example of `auditctl`, this means that the regular access controls on Linux still apply—if the current user does not have the rights to access the files used by `auditctl`, then using `runcon` will not suffice.

Switching roles

When a role transition is needed for more than just a couple of commands, it is necessary to open a shell with the new role. This will ensure that the entire session is now running with the new role assigned to it. Every activity performed from within this session will then run with the target role.

How to do it...

Switching roles with `sudo` or `newrole` is done as follows:

1. Switching a role can be done using `sudo -i` or `sudo -s` if allowed by the `sudoers` file. If the `ROLE` and `TYPE` attributes are set, then the target shell will have the proper context assigned:

    ```
    ~$ id -Z
    dbadm_u:staff_r:staff_t:s0
    ~$ sudo -u postgres -i
    Password:
    ~$ id -Z
    dbadm_u:dbadm_r:dbadm_t:s0
    ```

2. Switching roles can also be done using `newrole`:

    ```
    ~$ newrole -r dbadm_r
    ```

How it works...

Getting a shell after switching roles is not all that different from executing commands. However, the SELinux policy might not allow running shells and regular binaries in the target domain. For instance, a user who is allowed the `puppetca_t` domain through some role will not be able to run a shell in this domain, as `puppetca_t` is not allowed to be used through a shell—it is a domain for a particular set of commands.

Most user roles have a default user domain associated with them. The default user domain for a `dbadm_r` role is `dbadm_t`; the default domain for a `webadm_r` role is `webadm_t`. These user domains do have the privileges to be used through a shell.

The `newrole` command only requires the target role, as it will check the default type of a role (which is documented in the `default_type` file inside `/etc/selinux/mcs/contexts/`) and use this as the target type.

Creating a new role

Roles are part of SELinux policies. In order to create a new role, it isn't possible to just invoke a few `semanage` commands. Instead, an SELinux policy module will need to be created.

How to do it...

The SELinux policy needs to be updated in order to create a new role. The following steps can be used to do just that:

1. Create a new policy module named after the role to be created, such as `pgsqladm` (for a PostgreSQL administration role).

2. In the policy module, call the `userdom_login_user_template` interface:

   ```
   userdom_login_user_template(pgsqladm)
   ```

3. Assign the proper privileges to the `pgsqladm_r` role and `pgsqladm_t` type:

   ```
   postgresql_admin(pgsqladm_t, pgsqladm_r)
   ```

4. Edit the `default_type` file in `/etc/selinux/mcs/contexts/` to make `pgsqladm_t` the default type for the `pgsqladm_r` role:

   ```
   pgsqladm_r:pgsqladm_t
   ```

5. Edit the `default_contexts` file in `/etc/selinux/mcs/contexts/` to inform the system to which types a transition has to be made when a user switch is triggered by an application. For instance, for a local login session, the following code can be used for this purpose:

   ```
   system_r:local_login_t  user_r:user_t … pgsqladm_r:pgsqladm_t …
   ```

6. Now, build and load the policy, and verify that the new role is available:

   ```
   ~# seinfo -r | grep pgsqladm_r
   ```

How it works...

Creating new roles for an SELinux system requires changes on multiple levels. Updating the SELinux policy is just one of these.

Defining a role in the policy

The first step is to create a new role and user domain through the SELinux policy. There are a couple of templates available in the reference policy to easily build new roles. The relation between these templates is visualized in the following diagram:

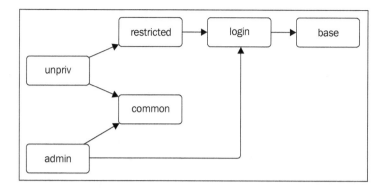

The various blocks in the diagram represent the following templates:

▶ In `userdom_base_user_template`, the basic rules and privileges for roles and user domains are documented, regardless of their future use. If a role needs to be declared with an absolute minimum of privileges, the use of this template is preferred.

▶ Inside `userdom_login_user_template`, `userdom_base_user_template` is called and extended with privileges related to interactive logins. When a role is created that is meant to be logged on directly (without the need to call `newrole` or `sudo`), then this interface is needed.

▶ Within `userdom_restricted_user_template`, the `userdom_login_user_template` interface is called, but the user domain is also associated with the `unpriv_userdomain` attribute, meant for end user domains that have little security impact on the system.

▶ The `userdom_common_user_template` interface adds privileges and rules that are common for both unprivileged and privileged roles.

▶ The `userdom_unpriv_user_template` interface calls both `userdom_common_user_template` and `userdom_restricted_user_template` and is meant to declare unprivileged roles and user domains with interactive logon and general system access.

▶ The `userdom_admin_user_template` interface calls both `userdom_common_user_template` and `userdom_login_user_template`, and creates a role and user domain that is meant to be used for administrative purposes.

Whenever such an appropriate interface is called, the proper role and type is created and can be used in the remainder of the policy module.

Extending the role privileges

In the example, we assigned PostgreSQL administrative rights to the `pgsqladm_t` user domain and allowed the `pgsqladm_r` role the proper PostgreSQL domains (if any).

The reference policy tends to provide two types of interfaces that can be assigned to new roles:

> ▸ Administrative roles, whose interface name usually ends with `_admin`
>
> ▸ End user roles, whose interface name usually ends with `_role` or `_run`

Administrative roles allow for rights on all resources related to a particular domain. In case of the `postgresql_admin` interface, the role and user domain (which are passed on to the interface) are allowed to send signals to the PostgreSQL services, execute the `init` script (to launch or shut down the service), and manage the various resources of the domain (such as the database files, configuration files, and logs).

Services almost always have an `_admin` interface. These are called after the domain, such as `puppet_admin` for Puppet administration and `samba_admin` for Samba administration. Sometimes, an SELinux policy module has multiple administrative interfaces when there are different domains involved. An example would be the `logging_admin_audit` and `logging_admin_syslog` interfaces, as both auditing and system logging are provided by the same SELinux policy module, but the administration of these two services can be segregated.

End user roles allow the user to execute client applications or interact with services. Such interfaces, such as `puppet_run_puppetca` (which allows a user domain to run the `puppetca` application and transition to it) and `openvpn_run` (which allows users to run OpenVPN services), can still be somewhat administrative in nature, so make sure to validate the content of the interface. However, most of the time, this is governed through the application side and not infrastructure side—being able to launch VPN services does not mean that the user can manipulate routing tables as they see fit, even though the VPN service domain (`openvpn_t`) can.

It is important to review the interfaces before blindly granting them to new roles and users. In case of PostgreSQL, the `postgresql_role` role, for instance, does not allow the user to interact with the PostgreSQL service; instead, the interface is used to support SEPostgreSQL (SELinux-enabled PostgreSQL), which provides additional access controls in PostgreSQL based on SELinux policies. When users are assigned the `postgresql_role` role, they are granted basic privileges inside a PostgreSQL environment.

To allow users to interact with PostgreSQL, the `postgresql_stream_connect` and `postgresql_tcp_connect` interfaces can be used.

Default types and default contexts

The `default_types` file informs SELinux what the default type is if no context is specified otherwise, and it is used by commands such as `newrole` to know what the default type is for a user.

The default_contexts file (which can be overridden through SELinux user-specific files in the users/ subdirectory) informs the SELinux libraries and subsystem what specific SELinux type to transition to when a user and role switch has occurred from within a specified domain. For instance, a cron daemon runs in the system_r:crond_t context, but when it executes the user cron jobs, these jobs themselves need to run in a different SELinux role and SELinux type. The following default_contexts configuration snippet would have the jobs of a user (whose role is pgsqladm_r) run as cronjob_t (rather than pgsqladm_t):

```
system_r:crond_t   pgsqladm_r:cronjob_t
```

These files are generated as part of the base policy. Sadly, there are no default_types. local or default_contexts.local files that can be used to provide system-specific changes. As a result, updates on the base SELinux policy might overwrite these files depending on how the Linux distribution treats these files. If the files are seen as configuration files (such as with Gentoo Linux), then they are not altered by system updates; instead, the system administrator is informed that an update on these files might be needed, keeping the manual changes made by the administrator in the past.

Initial role based on entry

Users will often have multiple roles associated with them. Depending on how they interact with the system, a different initial role (and a user domain) might be needed. Consider a user who interacts with a system locally (through the console), remotely through SSH (for administrative purposes), and through FTP (as an end user), as depicted in the following diagram:

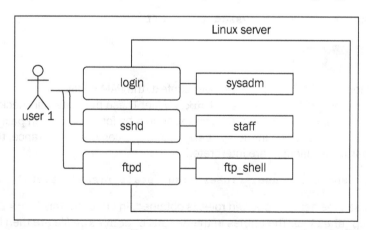

We want to make sure that the default role in which the user session starts on the system depends on the entry point on the system. Direct console logon can be in the administrative role, sysadm_r, whereas remote logon is first in the staff_r role (to ensure a stolen SSH key cannot be used to perform administrative tasks on the system without knowing the users' system password). The use of the FTP server should result in an unprivileged role, ftp_shell_r.

The ftp_shell_r role is a nondefault role and will not be available by default. Using SELinux with an FTP server in this setup requires that the FTP server is either SELinux aware (and supports context transitions) or uses PAM for its authentication rather than internal user accounts.

How to do it...

To configure the role to be used when a user logs on or starts a session, execute the following steps:

1. First of all, make sure that the user is assigned the various roles:

   ```
   ~# semanage user -m -R "staff_r sysadm_r ftp_shell_r" staff_u
   ```

2. Edit the default_contexts file by reordering the contexts, making sure that the right role is always mentioned before the others (or that the others are not mentioned at all):

   ```
   system_r:local_login_t:s0  user_r:user_t:s0  sysadm_r:sysadm_t:s0
   staff_r:staff_t:s0
   system_r:sshd_t:s0  user_r:user_t:s0  staff_r:staff_t:s0
   system_r:ftpd_t:s0  ftp_shell_r:ftp_shell_t:s0
   ```

3. Check whether the domains have support for specific Booleans that explicitly enable or disable transitioning into particular domains. For instance, consider the SSH daemon:

   ```
   ~# setsebool -P ssh_sysadm_login off
   ```

How it works...

When applications call PAM to set up the user context, the PAM configuration will invoke methods provided by the pam_selinux.so file. These methods will check the default_contexts file to see what the context should be for a user. When pam_selinux.so is loaded through a daemon in the system_r:sshd_t context, for instance, then the lines for that particular daemon are interpreted:

```
system_r:sshd_t:s0  user_r:user_t:s0  staff_r:staff_t:s0
```

For the given user, the set of supported roles is obtained. In our case, this is staff_r sysadm_r ftp_shell_r. The entries in the default_contexts file are then looked at one by one, and the first role that is mentioned in the default_contexts file, that is also an allowed role for the user, will be used.

In the given example, as user_r is not an allowed role, staff_r is the next one on the list. This role is allowed, so when the user logs on through SSH, then its default role will be the staff_r role (and its associated user domain will be staff_t).

Some domains are also configured to allow or disallow direct logins into administrative roles. The SSH policy, for instance, uses an SELinux Boolean called `ssh_sysadm_login`, which allows transitioning into any user (`ssh_sysadm_login=on`) or only to unprivileged users (`ssh_sysadm_login=off`), specified policy-wise as follows:

```
tunable_policy(`ssh_sysadm_login',`
  userdom_spec_domtrans_all_users(sshd_t)
  userdom_signal_all_users(sshd_t)
',`
  userdom_spec_domtrans_unpriv_users(sshd_t)
  userdom_signal_all_users(sshd_t)
')
```

A similar approach can easily be built into custom policies. Note that the use of `userdom_spec_domtrans_unpriv_users` will only allow using the daemon for roles and types created through `userdom_unpriv_user_template`, as this interface assigns the `unpriv_userdomain` attribute that is used by the `userdom_spec_domtrans_unpriv_users` interface.

Defining role transitions

It is possible to have SELinux automatically switch roles when a certain application is executed. The usual checks still apply (such as if the role is a valid one for the user, does the current user domain have execute rights, and many more), but then, there is no longer a need to call `runcon` or `sudo` to switch the role.

How to do it...

Role transitions can be configured as follows:

1. Identify the executable type on which a role transition has to occur:

   ```
   ~$ ls -Z puppetca
   system_u:object_r:puppetca_exec_t   puppetca
   ```

2. In the SELinux policy, create an interface that includes the role transitions:

   ```
   interface(`puppet_roletrans_puppetca',`
     gen_require(`
       role puppetadm_r;
       type puppetca_t, puppetca_exec_t;
     ')
     allow $1 puppetadm_r;
     role_transition $1 puppetca_exec_t puppetadm_r;
     domtrans_pattern($2, puppetca_exec_t, puppetca_t)
   ')
   ```

3. Assign the newly created interface to the user:

```
puppet_roletrans_puppetca(staff_r, staff_t)
```

How it works...

The first rule that is activated is a role-allow rule. Such a rule tells SELinux what role switch is allowed and in which direction. The set of allowed role switches can be queried using `sesearch`:

~# sesearch --role_allow

Consider the following role-allow rule(s) for the `puppetadm_r` role:

```
allow staff_r puppetadm_r
```

In this case, *only* the `staff_r` role is allowed to switch to the `puppetadm_r` role. Switching from the `puppetadm_r` role back to the `staff_r` role is not allowed.

The second rule tells SELinux that if a `puppetca_exec_t` labeled file is executed by the selected role (`staff_r`, in our case), then the role should switch to `puppetadm_r`. Of course, this is only done when the SELinux user is allowed the target role.

The third rule will perform a domain transition from `staff_t` to `puppetca_t` if `staff_t` executes a `puppetca_exec_t` labeled file.

It should be noted though that a forced role transition (that is, through the SELinux policy) is not a preferred method in the majority of cases, as it doesn't provide any flexibility to the administrator. If this is implemented, then using multiple roles is more difficult as some domains are hardcoded to a particular role.

Looking into access privileges

To finish off, let's look at how to verify access privileges granted to users. Specifying roles and privileges allows users to do their job, but from a security point of view, it is also important to verify if (and which) users can manipulate certain resources. Auditors will want to have an overview of who is able to, say, manipulate SELinux policies or read private keys.

How to do it...

To properly investigate access rights, the following approach can help in identifying users (and processes) that have the permissions we want to be informed about:

1. Verify file permissions that are not related to SELinux.

2. Verify direct access to the resource (such as read rights on private keys).

3. Look at who (users or applications) has the right to manipulate the SELinux policy.

4. Check users and domains that are granted direct access to filesystems and raw devices.

5. See when memory can be accessed directly.

6. Review who can update authentication files.

7. Analyze who can boot the system.

How it works...

Reviewing access is a lengthy process. It isn't sufficient to just look into file ownership (user and group) and look at the permissions of the file to find out who is actually able to read or modify the file (assuming that the privilege looked into is file access). Privilege delegation tools such as `sudo` (through the `sudoers` file or the `sudo` configuration in an LDAP server) need to be checked as well, together with the `setuid` application access, backup file access (when read access is to be examined), and more.

With the mandatory access controls that SELinux provides, checking the policy for access rights is an important part of such an evaluation. The `sesearch` application can assist in this quest.

Direct access inspection

To check direct access, we need to query both the access rights (such as write privileges on the resource) as well as relabeling rights. After all, a domain that is allowed to change the SELinux context of a file to another resource can theoretically switch the context, modify the file, and reset the context.

```
~# sesearch -t lvm_etc_t -c file -p write -ACST
Found 6 semantic av rules:
  allow sysadm_t non_auth_file_type : file { … };
  allow portage_t file_type : file { … };
...
~# sesearch -t lvm_etc_t -c file -p relabelfrom,relabelto -ACST
Found 5 semantic av rules:
  allow sysadm_t non_auth_file_type : file { … };
  allow restorecond_t non_auth_file_type : file { … };
  allow setfiles_t file_type : file { … };
…
```

This code shows not only the user domains that have the privileges, but also the application domains. In a review of permissions, it is necessary to also validate who can access and manipulate processes that run in these domains. This can be done by checking the transition permission:

```
~# sesearch -t setfiles_t -c process -p transition -ACST
```

For each of the domains, studying who can manipulate these processes is a time-consuming process and requires intimate knowledge of the application(s) that run in the given domain. For instance, the `restorecond` daemon will only reset file contexts to the context known by the SELinux tools (so, modifying the context temporarily is not possible through `restorecond`) and only on those locations that are configured in the `restorecond` configuration file.

Policy manipulation

Checking the SELinux policy isn't sufficient as the policy can be manipulated as well. Loading a new policy is governed through, among various other privileges, the `load_policy` permission:

```
~# sesearch -t security_t -c security -p load_policy -ACS
Found 2 semantic av rules:
EF allow kernel_t security_t : security load_policy  ;
  [ secure_mode_policyload ]
EF allow load_policy_t security_t : security load_policy ;
  [ secure_mode_policyload ]
```

Similarly, the access towards the selected domains (and the `load_policy_t` domain in particular) needs to be verified.

As can be seen from the output, manipulating the SELinux policy can also be controlled through an SELinux Boolean called `secure_mode_policyload`. When this Boolean is enabled, loading a new policy is no longer possible. If this Boolean is enabled and persisted, then even rebooting a system will not help unless the system is booted in the permissive mode.

Similarly, checking who can put the system in the permissive mode can be verified as well:

```
~# sesearch -p setenforce -ACS
```

This is governed through the same SELinux Boolean though.

Another way to manipulate the SELinux policy would be to boot the system in the permissive mode or even with SELinux disabled. This means that reviewing access to the boot files is also important (the `boot_t` type).

Indirect access

It is also possible to access resources indirectly, for instance, by manipulating the raw devices (such as disk devices or memory). Access to device files is already quite privileged on Linux systems. With SELinux, additional controls might be put in place.

Disk devices are usually labeled as `fixed_disk_device_t`. Access to these files should only be granted to application domains, although some privileged user domains might be able to relabel such device nodes or manipulate application domains to perform actions not granted to the regular user.

```
~# sesearch -t fixed_disk_device_t -ACS
```

Users who are able to manipulate files related to system authentication can grant themselves different user roles, for instance, by logging on to the system as a different user (who does have the rights needed). This includes access to `/etc/pam.d/` (usually labeled as `etc_t`) or the authentication libraries themselves in `/lib/security/` (usually labeled as `lib_t`).

7
Choosing the Confinement Level

In this chapter, we will cover the following recipes:

- ► Finding common resources
- ► Defining common helper domains
- ► Documenting common privileges
- ► Granting privileges to all clients
- ► Creating a generic application domain
- ► Building application-specific domains using templates
- ► Using fine-grained application domain definitions

Introduction

During the development of additional policies, developers can opt to use a very fine-grained policy model, a domain-per-application model, or a coarse-grained, functionality-based policy model. The relationship between these confinement models is shown in the following diagram:

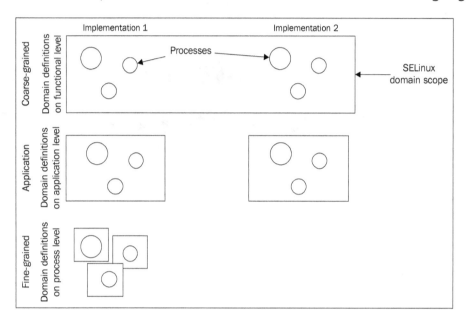

In very fine-grained policies, multiple domains are defined, so functionally different processes of the same application are all running in their own specialized SELinux domain. A coarse-grained policy, on the other hand, allows to have different applications with a similar functionality run with the same context. Application-level policies are somewhere in the middle: they focus on one domain (or a very small set of domains) for one application.

Most policies are developed using a **one domain per application** principle. Still, the choice of development patterns in policy development reflects the confinement level of an application, as shared, coarse-grained policies might allow for more interaction between applications and resources than intended, whereas, a fine-grained policy is much harder to develop and maintain.

When we look at a functional level, we usually focus on shared resources or resources that cannot be tied to a particular application. An example is the mta SELinux policy, which manages the main infrastructure-related shared content such as e-mail aliases (etc_mail_t), user mailboxes (mail_home_rw_t), e-mail spool files (mail_spool_t), and more.

Finding common resources

During policy development, some of the resources used by the policy are or could be shared with other policies. If that is the case, a functionality-driven policy module is created in which those common resources are placed. This allows other policies to use these resources and assign the right permissions through the interfaces declared in the functionality-driven policy.

How to do it...

Most of the work in this recipe is to figure out what resources are shared. This is done by completing the following steps:

1. Look for common files and directories that might be shared with other applications and whose ownership is not specifically tied to an application, but is more functional in nature. For these resources, declare them in a functionality-driven policy.

2. Check whether there are devices used that are functionally related to the policy but not to a specific application in particular.

3. Validate if there is specific user-provided content that is functionally related but not tied to a particular application, and where the default user content types (such as `user_home_t`) are better not used. These resources need to be declared in the functionality-driven policy and probably made customizable as well:

    ```
    type public_content_t; # customizable
    files_type(public_content_t)
    ```

4. Create the proper interfaces to handle or interact with these common resources:

    ```
    interface(`miscfiles_read_public_files',`
      gen_require(`
        type public_content_t;
      ')
      read_files_pattern($1, public_content_t, public_content_t)
    ')
    ```

How it works...

Functionality-driven policy modules handle common resources for multiple applications and policies. Some example policies that handle the functional resources for multiple applications are the mail transfer agent policy (`mta`) and the web server policy (`apache`). Although the web server policy was originally intended to be purely for the Apache HTTPd, it has since evolved into a more functionality-driven policy supporting a large amount of web server technologies.

Shared file locations

A helpful method for finding out what resources are considered to be functional in nature (rather than application-specific) is to imagine switching one application in favor of another. What resource types would remain the same if we switch from one system logger (say syslog-ng) to another (say rsyslog), or from Courier-IMAP to Cyrus? Having knowledge of multiple similar applications helps in finding out where (or what) the shared locations are.

However, having similar functional requirements doesn't necessarily make them shared. The locations should also remain the same (or at least be consistent and on well-known locations). Consider database files: the database files for PostgreSQL and SQLite databases both have the same functional purpose, but it makes no sense to label them both with the same label. Database files are specific to a particular database implementation and require specific labels, so with every potential common resource, make sure that the resource itself can be shared across multiple implementations.

Device nodes are a nice example to consider for a functionality-driven policy. An example device type definition would look like the following:

```
type cachefiles_device_t;
dev_node(cachefiles_device_t)
```

Devices are usually shared across multiple applications. Most devices are defined in the devices.te policy module with the proper interfaces being declared to allow access to the device (such as dev_rw_cachefiles for read/write access to the previously mentioned cachefiles_device_t type). Not all files in /dev/ are such device files though.

Consider the /dev/log socket, which is used to send log events to the system logger. This socket, which is available regardless of the system logger being used, is made available through the following logging SELinux policy module:

```
type devlog_t;
files_type(devlog_t)
mls_trusted_object(devlog_t)
```

The mls_trusted_object interface makes the device (labeled devlog_t) accessible for all security levels in an MLS-enabled policy.

User content and customizable types

User-provided content is also important to consider. For instance, for e-mail-related daemons, a user's .forward file (which tells the system where to forward the e-mails of the user) is available in his or her home directory and is definitely not owned by a particular application. Hence, its label (mail_home_t) is tied to a functionality-driven policy (mta).

Don't forget to mark user content as user content through the `userdom_user_home_content` interface; otherwise, end users will not be able to label or manipulate these files:

```
type mail_home_t;
userdom_user_home_content(mail_home_t)
```

Some user content is also best marked as customizable. A **customizable type**, when assigned to a resource, is ignored during standard relabel operations (usually performed by the system administrator) and as such, the resource label will not be changed back to what the SELinux configuration files have defined. This is particularly useful for resources whose path is not a fixed location and usually not made part of the SELinux file context definitions.

If the administrator does a forced relabel operation, then the file context is reset, even if the current type assigned to the resource is a customizable type:

```
~# restorecon -R -F /home/*
```

In a modular policy development, there is no notation available to mark a type as being a customizable type. To do this, the type needs to be added to the `customizable_types` file in `/etc/selinux/mcs/contexts/`.

Marking files with a customizable type is a solution when the path of the resource isn't fixed. The `.forward` file has a fixed path, so there is no need for customizable content. User content that should be publicly accessible, however, (marked as `public_content_t` or `public_content_rw_t`) does not have a fixed path; hence, those types are (by default) marked as customizable.

When full policy development is done (for instance, through the Linux distribution policy or because the developer controls the entire policy and not just additional modules), then the `# customizable` comment can be placed behind the type declaration, as can be seen from the following example of the CVS policy module:

```
type cvs_data_t; # customizable
files_type(cvs_data_t)
```

The reference policy build system will then automatically add the type to the `customizable_types` file during the build process.

There's more...

Other common resources that can be considered are the TCP and UDP ports. Indeed, network-facing applications bind to one or more ports, which are usually the same for applications sharing the same functionality.

However, the TCP and UDP ports cannot be declared inside SELinux policy modules; instead, they need to be labeled as part of the base policy. Updating a base policy, however, is either done by the Linux distribution maintainers or the upstream reference policy project. The basic rule is that the ports are named after the service they are generally used by:

```
~$ getent services 6667
ircd      6667/tcp
~$ seinfo --portcon=6667
portcon tcp 6667 system_u:object_r:ircd_port_t
```

Defining common helper domains

Next to the common resources, some applications share the same set of helper commands. The `sendmail` command is a nice example of this, which is executed by a large set of domains (usually, applications that need to send e-mails without using the SMTP protocol themselves). The `sendmail` application is well understood and most MTA applications support it for command-line e-mail sending operations.

Supporting such helper domains is usually done through a functionality-driven policy.

How to do it...

Creating helper domains is similar to creating regular application domains, but the use of attributes allows the policy to be very flexible and usable by the application-specific policy modules developed further. Let's look at the MTA definition as an example of how this can be accomplished:

1. Define an attribute for the command type:
   ```
   attribute mta_exec_type;
   ```

2. Create a proper label type for the command, and assign it the `mta_exec_type` attribute:
   ```
   type sendmail_exec_t, mta_exec_type;
   application_executable_file(sendmail_exec_t);
   ```

3. Configure an application domain for the command:
   ```
   type system_mail_t;
   application_domain(system_mail_t, sendmail_exec_t)
   ```

4. If the application is for system purposes, assign the domain to the `system_r` role:
   ```
   role system_r types system_mail_t
   ```

5. If the application is meant to be executed by end users, do not forget to include a `_run` or `_role` interface.

6. Make an interface callable by third-party application domains to allow them to interact with the helper application:

```
interface(`mta_send_mail',`
  gen_require(`
    attribute mta_exec_type;
    type system_mail_t;
  ')
  corecmd_search_bin($1)
  domtrans_pattern($1, mta_exec_type, system_mail_t)
')
```

7. Make another interface allowing specific policies to mark their own helper executables usable for the same purpose (as they might not always use the same type):

```
interface(`mta_agent_executable',`
  gen_require(`
    attribute mta_exec_type;
  ')
  typeattribute $1 mta_exec_type;
  application_executable_file($1)
')
```

How it works...

Helper domains are meant to provide reusable functionality across multiple implementations. To support the flexibility of having multiple implementations, attributes are usually assigned to the types so that extensions can be easily created.

Consider the `sendmail` example again. Most implementations will have the command-line `sendmail` application marked as `sendmail_exec_t`. However, there are implementations whose `sendmail` binary has many more features, especially when called from the implementation processes themselves. Some implementations even have the file as a symbolic link to a more generic e-mail-handler application.

The Exim implementation, for instance, uses `exim_exec_t` instead of using `sendmail_exec_t`. With the use of the attributes, the Exim policy module can just call the proper interface (`mta_agent_executable`, in this case), so third-party applications can still execute the command (even though it is `exim_exec_t` and not `sendmail_exec_t`) and have it behave as expected (that is, with a transition to the `user_mail_t` or `system_mail_t` domain as expressed by the MTA policy):

```
type exim_exec_t;
mta_mailserver(exim_t, exim_exec_t)
mta_agent_executable(exim_exec_t)
```

Attributes allow other domains to interact with the newly defined type without having to update the policy modules that define these domains. This is because those domains are granted execute rights on all types that have the `mta_exec_type` attribute assigned, and will invoke a domain transition to the `system_mail_t` helper domain when they execute such a file. This privilege is provided through the `mta_send_mail` interface, which is a good example of a helper domain interface to be assigned to other domains:

```
interface(`mta_send_mail',`
  gen_require(`
    type system_mail_t;
    attribute mta_exec_type;
  ')
  corecmd_search_bin($1)
  domtrans_pattern($1, mta_exec_type, system_mail_t)
  allow $1 mta_exec_type:lnk_file read_lnk_file_perms;
')
```

Documenting common privileges

Next to the helper domains, most functionality-driven policies also group privileges that can be assigned to domains. Such privileges could be to not only manage the common resources, but also to extend other domains with functional requirements as managed by the common policy.

All e-mail daemons need to be able to bind to the proper TCP ports, handle user mailboxes, and so on. By bundling these common privileges on the functional policy level, any evolution pertaining to the policy can be immediately granted to all domains inheriting privileges from the functional policy, rather than having to update each domain individually.

How to do it...

Common privileges can be found in a wide variety. How common privileges are assigned depends on the use case. The following method, based on the e-mail server definition in the MTA policy, provides a flexible approach to this:

1. Create an attribute for the functional domain to which common privileges are granted:

   ```
   attribute mailserver_domain;
   ```

2. Define an interface where the attribute is assigned to a specified domain:

   ```
   interface(`mta_mailserver',`
     gen_require(`
       attribute mailserver_domain;
     ')
     typeattribute $1 mailserver_domain;
   ')
   ```

3. Build an interface that assigns the functionally related common privileges to the specified argument. It should not assign attributes though! This is done with the following code:

```
interface(`mta_mailserver_privs,`
  gen_require(`
    type mail_home_t;
  ')
  allow $1 mail_home_t:file read_file_perms;

  ...
')
```

4. Now, use the newly created interface to grant the proper permissions on the attribute:

```
mta_mailserver_privs(mailserver_domain)
```

5. If a specific application always has to inherit the privileges, assign the attribute to it:

```
mta_mailserver(exim_t)
```

6. If a specific application, however, optionally inherits the privileges, use the domain interface:

```
tunable_policy(`nginx_enable_mailproxy',`
  mta_mailserver_privs(nginx_t)
')
```

How it works...

When assigning privileges to a domain, there are two approaches that can be taken: either the privileges are assigned to an attribute (which is then associated with a domain) or the privileges are directly assigned to the domain. Which one to pick depends on how the policy is going to be used. Due to restrictions in policy development, it is not possible to optionally (that is, triggered through SELinux Booleans) assign attributes. Any attempt to do so will result in a build failure, as follows:

```
~$ make mymodule.pp
Compiling mcs mymodule module
checkmodule: loading policy configuration from tmp/mymodule.tmp
mymodule.te:23:ERROR 'syntax error' at token 'typeattribute'
on line 1309:
#line 23
   typeattribute $1 mta_exec_type;
checkmodule: error(s) encountered while parsing configuration
```

As a result, whenever permissions can be granted optionally (through SELinux Booleans), policy developers will have to make sure that the permissions are granted directly (instead of assigning an attribute to the domain).

However, in most cases, using attributes for domains makes sense. The policy itself does not increase in size that much (as rules remain on an attribute level) and administrators can easily query which domains participate in the functional approach:

```
~# seinfo -amailserver_domain -x
  mailserver_domain
    system_mail_t
    exim_t
    courier_smtpd_t
```

Granting the permissions through an interface also allows us to quickly look at the impact of assigning an attribute, as we can then use the `seshowif` command:

```
~$ seshowif mta_mailserver_privs
```

The example given uses a server-domain approach, but the same can be done for a client.

Granting privileges to all clients

The approach of using interfaces to aggregate privileges not only benefits domains that have the same functional purpose, but also clients. By combining the privileges for the set of clients, it is possible to enhance client privileges by only updating the interface rather than having to update all the clients' policy modules.

How to do it...

Create a client interface that can be assigned to all clients of a particular functional purpose. The following steps extend an example policy with antimalware support:

1. In the antimalware generic policy, create an `avcheck_client` attribute:

   ```
   attribute avcheck_client;
   ```

2. Create the interface that assigns the attribute to a client domain:

   ```
   interface(`av_check_client',`
     gen_require(`
       attribute avcheck_client;
     ')
     typeattribute $1 avcheck_client;
   ')
   ```

3. Create the interface that assigns the common privileges for client domains:

```
interface(`av_check_client_privs',`

  ...

')
```

4. In the created interface, add the privileges that need to be assigned to all client domains. For instance, to enable a domain transition for the ClamAV `check` command, the following code is used:

```
optional_policy(`
  clamav_domtrans_check($1)
')
```

5. All domains that act as a client are either assigned the `av_check_client` (if the attribute can be assigned) or `av_check_client_privs` interface.

How it works...

Suppose a new antimalware policy is developed for ClamAV, and we want the clients to be able to execute the `clamav_check_exec_t` applications and transition them to the `clamav_check_t` domain. Instead of updating all clients with a `clamav_domtrans_check` call, we only do this in the generic antimalware policy's `av_check_client_privs` interface, as follows:

```
optional_policy(`
  clamav_domtrans_check($1)
')
```

This ensures that all proper domains— not only those with the `avcheck_client` attribute—get the necessary privileges assigned.

Another example that uses this principle is the PulseAudio policy. An interface called `pulseaudio_client_domain` is made available and should be used by PulseAudio clients. Whenever the permissions for a PulseAudio client need to be updated, then the policy developer only needs to update the `pulseaudio_client_domain` interface instead of all client policy modules.

Such an approach makes policy development much more flexible and efficient, as developers do not need to update all possible client domains with the added privileges.

Creating a generic application domain

In some situations, it makes sense to create a generic application domain, even though multiple implementations exist for the same functionality. Examples are the Java domain (which works for all the popular Java™ implementations) and init domain. When this occurs, carefully consider whether the generic application domain will always be sufficient, or whether specific application domains might come into play later. When this isn't clear, make sure that the policy being developed is flexible enough to cater both situations.

How to do it...

In order to create a generic application policy that is still flexible with respect to potential specific policies that would be developed later, follow the upcoming set of steps:

1. Identify the permissions that are (almost) always applicable to the functional domain, regardless of the implementation.

2. Assign those permissions to a *base* implementation. For instance, for Java™ implementations, assign permissions as follows:

```
attribute javadomain;
# Minimal permissions
java_base_runtime_domain(javadomain);

type java_t;
# Assigns javadomain attribute
java_base_runtime(java_t);
```

3. Add permissions that are applicable to at least one (or a few) of the implementations to the standard type. In our example, this would be to java_t. This ensures that java_t is generally usable for most Java™ implementations.

4. Add the proper file contexts to allow most implementations to benefit from the generic application policy:

```
/usr/lib/bin/java[^/]*  --
  gen_context(system_u:object_r:java_exec_t,s0)
/opt/(.*/)?bin/java[^/]*  --
  gen_context(system_u:object_r:java_exec_t,s0)
```

How it works...

With the given implementation, most Java™ implementations on an SELinux-enabled system will run, when executed, in the generic `java_t` domain: their executables are all marked as `java_exec_t` through generic file context expressions, and the `java_t` domain holds not only the set of least privileges for Java™ domains (as granted through the `javadomain` attribute that gets them from the `java_base_runtime_privs` interface), but also those privileges that are common for quite a few implementations. This means that the `java_t` domain has more privileges than needed in most cases, as it has to support a broad set of Java™ implementations.

However, when a specific implementation will be created with a different policy profile than the existing `java_t` domain, policy developers can easily mark this domain as a Java domain, inheriting the permissions that are necessary for every Java™ implementation (for instance, because they are mandated through the specifications of Java™) while staying clear from the other permissions that are granted to the generic `java_t` domain:

```
type icedtea_java_t;
java_base_runtime(icedtea_java_t)
```

By creating a more specific file context definition, the executable of the newly created type will get this label assigned (as the other expressions are more generic, and the SELinux utilities use a *most specific definition first* approach):

```
/opt/icedtea7/bin/java  --
   gen_context(system_u:object_r:icedtea_java_exec_t,s0)
```

Building a proper set of least privilege rules is not easy and requires experience in policy development. If uncertain, it might be a good idea to use SELinux Booleans, such as used by the (generic) `cron` policy:

```
# Support extra rules for fcron
gen_tunable(fcron_crond, false)
...
tunable_policy(`fcron_crond',`
  allow admin_crontab_t self:process setfscreate;
')
```

Through this approach, specific implementations can still benefit from the generic policy declaration, if the amount of additional permissions is small. As the policy is enhanced with other implementation details, the need for the `tunable_policy` statement might be removed or a specific implementation for `fcron` can be developed separately.

Building application-specific domains using templates

Specific domains have the advantage that they can contain those privileges needed by the domain, and no more. As there are no other application implementations using the specific domain, the privileges can be tailored to the needs of the application.

In certain situations though, it might be beneficial to automatically generate the types together with the basic permissions. Generating types is done through templates (rather than interfaces, although the underlying implementation of interfaces and templates is quite similar). The approach and development method is aligned with interface definitions and should pose no difficulties for developers to understand.

An example to consider with templates would be to automatically create system `cron` job domains for individual applications. Through a template, we can automatically create the domain, executable type, and temporary resource types as well as properly document the interactions of that domain with the main `cron` daemon (which is needed for communicating job failures or success, handling output, logging, and so on).

How to do it...

Creating templates is similar to creating interfaces. To create templates, the following approach can be used:

1. Start with a skeleton template inside the `.if` file, but call it `template` instead of `interface`:

    ```
    template(`cron_system_job_template',`
      ...
    ')
    ```

2. Add in the following type declarations:

    ```
    type $1_cronjob_t;
    type $1_cronjob_exec_t;
    application_domain($1_cronjob_t, $1_cronjob_exec_t)

    type $1_cronjob_tmp_t;
    files_tmp_file($1_cronjob_tmp_t)
    ```

3. Grant the proper interactions between the main daemon and the newly defined types that are still inside the template definition:

    ```
    allow crond_t $1_cronjob_t:fd use;
    allow crond_t $1_cronjob_t:key manage_key_perms;
    domtrans_pattern(crond_t, $1_cronjob_exec_t, $1_cronjob_t)
    ...
    ```

4. In the application policy, call the template so that the new types are created. For instance, to create the `cron` job domains for Puppet, add the following code to `puppet.te`:

```
cron_system_job_template(puppet)
```

5. Enhance the (now available) `puppet_cronjob_t` domain with the permissions needed:

```
allow puppet_cronjob_t …
```

How it works...

The use of templates has been discussed earlier in the chapter on web server content. Indeed, the `apache_content_template` definition, too, is a template that creates additional types and documents the interaction between the newly created types and the (main) web server domain.

The use of templates allows for rapid policy development as well as properly isolated permission handling. When the main application evolves and requires additional permissions with respect to the specific application domains, or certain permissions are no longer needed, then only the template needs to be adjusted. All that is needed to apply the changes is to rebuild the SELinux policy modules, without any need to alter their individual source files.

It is a best practice to use prefix and/or suffix notations for template-provided types and to end the name of the template with `_template`. In theory, it is perfectly possible to create a template that creates the specified type(s) without any prefix and postfix expressions, instead requiring the various types to be passed on one at a time:

```
cron_system_job_template(puppet_cronjob_t, puppet_cronjob_exec_t,
puppet_cronjob_tmp_t)
```

However, this approach is inflexible under the following circumstances:

▸ If additional types need to be supported, then the interface API itself (the number of arguments passed to it and their meaning) needs to be altered, which makes such changes incompatible with earlier releases. This is important because there might be policy developers who are using this interface without their policy being available in the repository that we're developing in, so we cannot refactor this code ourselves.

▸ If a type is no longer needed, then either the interface API itself needs to be changed (making it incompatible with earlier releases) or the interface will be made to ignore a particular type (which easily becomes a development nightmare).

▸ Developers will continuously need to look at the order and meaning of the types in order not to mistakenly have the executable type marked as a domain and vice versa.

Such an approach would also make it possible to create confusing type definitions:

```
cron_system_job_template(puppetjob_t, pj_exec_t, ptmp_t)
```

Through such an approach, developers and administrators would lose sight over the relation between types.

Using proper prefix and postfix notations allows for a simplified management. The use of a template such as `cron_system_job_template` easily informs developers that there will be several types matching `*_cronjob_t`, `*_cronjob_exec_t`, and `*_cronjob_tmp_t`. Policy developers and system administrators easily learn that these are related with each other.

Using fine-grained application domain definitions

The use of templates earlier in this chapter is a start to support more fine-grained application domain definitions. Instead of running a workload inside the same domain as the main application, specific types are created that are meant to optimize the interaction between one domain and another, ensuring that the permissions granted to a particular domain remain small and manageable.

Using fine-grained application domains goes a step further, having processes of the same application run inside their own specific domains. This is not always possible (not all applications use multiple, distinct processes), but when it is, using fine-grained domains provides an even more secure environment, where each task runs with just the permissions needed for that individual task, even though the application, in general, needs more permissions.

An example implementation of fine-grained application domain definitions is the postfix policy, which will be used as an example in this recipe. The Postfix e-mail server is well documented and its architecture has been quite stable, making it a prime candidate for a fine-grained policy development approach.

However, when fine-grained application domains are used, policy development and maintenance itself becomes harder. Individual interaction changes between processes (which might be the case with newer versions of an application) require policy updates much more often than when all processes run within the same SELinux domain.

How to do it...

The following checks can be taken to see whether fine-grained application domains make sense or not:

1. Does the application architecture use multiple processes, with each process having a distinct functional task? If not, then creating fine-grained application domains will not help much as every domain will have the same permissions anyhow.

2. Are there processes with different access vectors (and thus are vulnerable to different threats than others)? For instance, whether some processes are directly accessible through the network whereas others are local? If so, then using fine-grained application domains might make sense to reduce the impact in case of the vulnerability exploitation.

3. Is there an interaction between a subset of the processes with other domains (not managed through the same application), whereas the other processes do not need to interact with these domains? If so, then using fine-grained application domains might make sense to limit exposure of resources to other applications.

4. Does the application support different roles that might need to interact with some (but not all) of the processes? A single full-application administrator might still need administrative privileges to all processes and resources, but other roles might not have this requirement. Using fine-grained application domains allows for fine-grained roles as well.

How it works...

Supporting fine-grained application domains is usually done for risk mitigation. But besides risk mitigation, it also provides advantages in role management as well as a more efficient approach to managing types that are inherited from the domain.

Reducing exploit risks

Consider a part of the Postfix architecture, as shown in the next diagram:

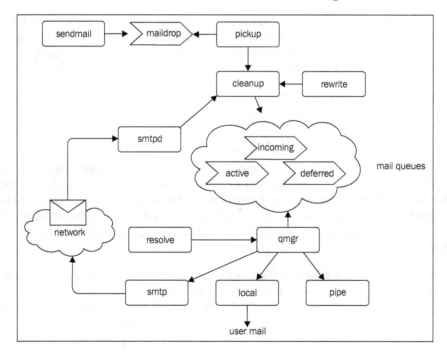

The **smtpd** daemon handles the reception of an e-mail through the **network**, and as such, is more prone to remote vulnerability exploits than to locally running processes such as the **cleanup** process or even the **qmgr** process.

By limiting resource access of the **smtpd** daemon to just the resources it needs, exploits that would attempt to access the queues (resources not usually accessed by **smtpd** but used by **qmgr**) would fail as the least privilege approach used in the **smtpd** domain (`postfix _smtpd_t`) disallows access to the **maildrop** queues (`postfix_spool_maildrop_t`).

Proper risk reduction is only possible if the resources of the application (such as the specific queues) are also defined in a fine-grained manner. If the application has multiple configuration files and these configuration files are read by different functional processes, then the configuration files should be labeled more specifically as well (for instance, configuration files for routing and configuration files for network settings).

If the application resources are labeled in a generic fashion, we risk that all fine-grained domains have the same rights towards the generic resources, making it more plausible for a vulnerable application to be exploited with larger consequences to the entire application architecture.

Role management

Using fine-grained application domains goes further than just mitigation of exploits. With individual domains, role access can be granted to users allowing them to take specific actions without requiring full application privileges.

For instance, operator roles can be created that allow manipulation of the Postfix deferred queue and signaling of the `qmgr` process without granting those users any specific rights towards the other processes. Assuming the user domain for this role is `postoper_t`, this would be accomplished as follows:

```
postfix_signal_qmgr(postoper_t)
postfix_manage_maildrop(postoper_t)
```

Type inheritance and transitions

When a domain creates new resources, these resources are assigned a type based on the label of the domain as well as the transitions defined in the SELinux policy. A process that is launched by a domain by default (that is, when no transitions are defined in the policy) inherits the label of the parent domain, while a file created inside a directory by default inherits the type of that parent directory. In the case of labeled network support, the packets are labeled based on the parent socket label.

Sometimes the creation of a resource cannot be tied to a parent domain or parent resource, making it impossible for SELinux to deduce the label to assign to this resource. For this reason, **initial SIDs** are provided by the SELinux policy. These tell the SELinux subsystem what the default label is for such resources if no label can be deduced.

For instance, the initial SIDs for a (TCP/UDP) port and for a file are as follows:

```
sid port gen_context(system_u:object_r:port_t,s0)
sid file gen_context(system_u:object_r:unlabeled_t,s0)
```

The definition of initial SIDs is part of the base SELinux policy and cannot be altered using SELinux policy modules. Luckily, there is little reason for SELinux developers to ever touch the initial SID definitions.

These label inheritance rules are important in a fine-grained application domain design. Applications that use multiple processes also tend to use resources such as shared memory for **inter-process communication** (**IPC**). When all processes run with the same domain, the shared memory is also labeled the same (such as `postgresql_tmpfs_t` for the PostgreSQL managed shared memory) as a file transition would be put in place:

```
# /dev/shm/ shared memory
type postgresql_$1_tmpfs_t;
files_tmpfs_file(postgresql_$1_tmpfs_t)
...
fs_tmpfs_filetrans(postgresql_$1_t, postgresql_$1_tmpfs_t, file)
```

When using multiple domain definitions, it is possible that shared memory segments are labeled differently as well (depending on which process creates the shared memory segments, of course), so even IPC can then be properly governed. Separate file transitions would be put in place depending on the domain that is creating a shared memory segment.

Next to file transitions, policy developers can also introduce domain transitions (which changes the label of the newly created process) using the `domtrans_pattern` definition. Inside the Postfix policy, this is used to create the fine-grained process architecture:

```
domtrans_pattern(postfix_master_t, postfix_postqueue_exec_t,
  postfix_postqueue_t)
domtrans_pattern(postfix_master_t, postfix_showq_exec_t,
  postfix_showq_t)
```

Such domain transitions can also be supported through the interfaces, as we've seen in the earlier chapters, such as the `postfix_domtrans_smtp` interface:

```
interface(`postfix_domtrans_smtp',`
  gen_require(`
    type postfix_smtp_t, postfix_smtp_exec_t;
  ')
  corecmd_search_bin($1)
  domtrans_pattern($1, postfix_smtp_exec_t, postfix_smtp_t)
')
```

A third transition type that SELinux supports is the dynamic domain transition. Such SELinux policy rules inform the SELinux subsystem that a process can change its own type dynamically—without needing to execute a file. This does require the application to be SELinux-aware (that is, be able to interact with the SELinux subsystem itself). For instance, inside the FTP policy, the following interface is made available to support domains dynamically transitioning to the `anon_sftpd_t` domain:

```
interface(`ftp_dyntrans_anon_ftpd',`
  gen_require(`
    type anon_sftpd_t;
  ')
  dyntrans_pattern($1, anon_sftpd_t)
')
```

In our Postfix example, we used the `/dev/shm/` shared memory, but there is also POSIX shared memory, which is governed through the `shm` class. This shared memory inherits the label from the domain itself, so if two applications (such as `postfix_pickup_t` and `postfix_cleanup_t`) use POSIX shared memory, then the target label is inherited from the process that creates the shared memory region:

```
allow postfix_pickup_t postfix_cleanup_t:shm rw_shm_perms;
```

Without fine-grained access controls, this would all be handled by a single domain (say `postfix_t`) and shared memory access controls would be very limited.

8

Debugging SELinux

In this chapter, we will look at SELinux debugging through the following recipes:

- ▸ Identifying whether SELinux is to blame
- ▸ Analyzing SELINUX_ERR messages
- ▸ Logging positive policy decisions
- ▸ Looking through SELinux constraints
- ▸ Ensuring an SELinux rule is never allowed
- ▸ Using strace to clarify permission issues
- ▸ Using strace against daemons
- ▸ Auditing system behavior

Introduction

On an SELinux-enabled system, the SELinux policy defines how applications should behave. Any change in behavior might trigger SELinux denials for certain actions of that application. As a result, end users can notice unexpected permission issues or erratic application behavior.

Troubleshooting such situations is usually done through analysis of the AVC events. Many resources already cover AVC events in great detail. The basic premise is that an AVC event uses a set of key-value pairs, as follows:

```
type=AVC msg=audit(1369306885.125:4702304): avc: denied { append }
    for pid=1787 comm="syslog-ng" name="oracle_audit.log" dev=dm-18
      ino=65 scontext=system_u:system_r:syslogd_t:s0
        tcontext=system_u:object_r:usr_t:s0 tclass=file
```

In this example, we can deduce the following from the AVC event:

▸ The event is a denial (`avc: denied`)

▸ The operation that was denied is appending to a file (`{ append }` ... `tclass=file`)

▸ The process that tried to append to the file has PID `1787` and name `syslog-ng` (`pid=1787 comm="syslog-ng"`)

▸ The process' context is `syslogd_t` (`scontext=system_u:system_r: syslogd_t:s0`)

▸ The target file is called `oracle_audit.log` and has an inode number `65` on the filesystem, stored on the `/dev/dm-18` metadevice (`name="oracle_audit.log" dev=dm-18 ino=65`)

▸ The file's context is `usr_t` (`tcontext=system_u:object_r:usr_t:s0`)

However, sometimes it isn't sufficient to find out where the problem is. Luckily, there are many more options available to debug the problem.

Identifying whether SELinux is to blame

Before blaming the SELinux subsystem and policies for a problem, it is important to verify whether SELinux is to blame at all. Too often, hours of troubleshooting are put in analyzing the SELinux policies and subsystem only to find out that the problem also persists when SELinux is not enabled.

How to do it...

In order to be confident that SELinux is (or isn't) to blame, the following set of steps can be taken:

1. Is it possible to get more information through the application's internal debugging system? Consider the following instance:

```
~# puppet master
Error: Could not find class puppet::agent for foo.bar on
node foo.bar
~# puppet master --debug --no-daemonize --verbose
```

2. Is an AVC denial related to the problem shown in the audit logs? If not, try disabling the `dontaudit` rules and try again:

```
~# semodule -DB
```

3. Is the application that gives problems SELinux-aware? Most SELinux-aware applications are linked with the `libselinux.so` library, so we can verify whether this is the case using `ldd` or `scanelf`:

    ```
    ~# ldd /usr/bin/dbus-daemon
            linux-vdso.so.1 =>  (0x00007fff56df4000)
            libexpat.so.1 => /lib64/libexpat.so.1 (0x00007f55710ae000)
            libselinux.so.1 => /lib64/libselinux.so.1
    (0x00007f5570e8f000)
            libaudit.so.1 => /lib64/libaudit.so.1 (0x00007f5570c72000)
            libcap-ng.so.0 => /lib64/libcap-ng.so.0
    (0x00007f5570a6d000)
            libpthread.so.0 => /lib64/libpthread.so.0
    (0x00007f5570850000)
            librt.so.1 => /lib64/librt.so.1 (0x00007f5570647000)
            libc.so.6 => /lib64/libc.so.6 (0x00007f55702b3000)
            libdl.so.2 => /lib64/libdl.so.2 (0x00007f55700af000)
            /lib64/ld-linux-x86-64.so.2 (0x0000003458000000)
    ```

4. Is the issue login related? If so, an application might not be SELinux-aware but still behave differently, as it uses PAM under the hood, which calls the `pam_selinux.so` library.

5. Does the problem still persist if the application domain is put in permissive mode? To check this, issue the following command:

    ```
    ~# semanage permissive -a portage_t
    ```

6. If the application domain is unknown, try putting the entire system in permissive mode (if allowed) to see whether the problem is still showing up. If it is, then SELinux might not be the cause after all:

    ```
    ~# setenforce 0
    ```

How it works...

Ensuring that SELinux is the cause of a problem is the first step to enlightenment. Numerous hours of SELinux investigations to resolve issues are spent only to find out that the problem was not with SELinux to begin with.

Getting more information from the application (or applications) involved is the first step to troubleshooting issues. Many applications have command-line flags that increase logging verbosity, and many daemons can be configured to log more of their inner workings. The resulting debug information (or even trace information, if the application supports it) will provide a massive help to the administrator to troubleshoot a problem.

If additional logging does not help, then it is important to verify whether there are AVC denials in the audit logs. As some AVC denials can be hidden during regular operations, disabling the `dontaudit` rules temporarily might be necessary. Don't stare blindly at AVC denials though, and take a broader look at logfiles and audit events. For instance, in the next recipe (*Analyzing SELINUX_ERR messages*), a more in-depth analysis of a particular audit event type is discussed.

Look through the various logs on the system as well. The output of `dmesg` is important if the problem is kernel, hardware, or core-system related. The `messages` logfile (in `/var/log/`) usually contains pointers when issues come up with system daemons.

When no denials are shown and there is no specific logging that can assist with the troubleshooting of an application, the next step is to assure ourselves that the application is not SELinux-aware.

SELinux-aware applications (applications that know they run on an SELinux-enabled system and interact with the SELinux subsystem) can act differently based on the SELinux policy that is loaded, without actually triggering any SELinux decision in the SELinux subsystem. On account of their awareness, the in-kernel SELinux subsystem access controls might not be called, so no logging will be shown even though the problem is somewhat SELinux-related.

Although there is not any 100 percent certain method to check whether an application is SELinux-aware, the two most common approaches are as follows:

- ▸ Checking whether the application binary is linked with the `libselinux.so` library
- ▸ Checking whether the application uses PAM

An application that is linked with the `libselinux.so` library is SELinux-aware and will be able to query SELinux policies, possibly acting differently when SELinux is enabled and often regardless of SELinux being in the enforcing or permissive mode.

Besides the `ldd` command, it is also possible to use the `scanelf` application as provided by the `pax-utils` package. This application does not need execute privileges against the binary (which `ldd` requires) but has the downside that it only shows the requirements for the binary, while `ldd` also includes the libraries linked by the libraries themselves:

```
~$ scanelf -n /usr/bin/dbus-daemon
 TYPE    NEEDED FILE
ET_DYN libexpat.so.1,libselinux.so.1,libaudit.so.1,libcap-ng.
so.0,libpthread.so.0,librt.so.1,libc.so.6 /usr/bin/dbus-daemon
```

Applications that use PAM can also be influenced by SELinux, since their PAM configuration might call the `pam_selinux.so` library (or not call it, which can be equally damaging for the functionality of the application as no transition will occur then, having the user session still run with the context of the daemon).

If the application does not interact with the SELinux subsystem to query the SELinux policy, and it also doesn't handle SELinux labels directly (that is, it has no knowledge of SELinux labels and does not actively work with them code-wise), then running the application in the permissive mode should show us whether SELinux is to blame. In the permissive mode, the SELinux subsystem access controls do not prevent any action. If a problem still persists in the permissive mode, chances are that SELinux is not to blame at all.

See also

> ▸ More information about SELinux-aware applications and how to write one is covered in *Chapter 10, Handling SELinux-aware Applications*

Analyzing SELINUX_ERR messages

When the SELinux subsystem is asked to perform an invalid SELinux-specific operation, it will log this through the audit subsystem using the `SELINUX_ERR` message type.

Getting ready

Make sure that the audit subsystem is up and running as we will be using the `ausearch` application to (re)view audit events:

```
~# service auditd start
```

How to do it...

Analyzing `SELINUX_ERR` messages is done by viewing the entry in the audit logs and understanding the individual fields; this is done by completing the following steps:

1. Note the current date/time, or reload the SELinux policy, to have a clear point in the audit logs from where to look:

   ```
   ~# semodule -R
   ```

2. Trigger the behavior in the application.

3. Ask the audit subsystem to show the last events of the `SELINUX_ERR` and `MAC_POLICY_LOAD` types:

   ```
   ~# ausearch -m SELINUX_ERR,MAC_POLICY_LOAD -ts recent
   ```

4. Look at the beginning of the message to find out what problematic situation SELinux is informing us about.

How it works...

The SELinux subsystem will log any incorrect request. If it is application behavior, it is usually logged through the AVC type; but when the request is SELinux-specific and incorrect, an `SELINUX_ERR` message type is displayed. In the example, we also looked for the `MAC_POLICY_LOAD` type, so we know at which stage the SELinux policy was reloaded, giving us a good starting point for the investigation.

Some examples of the `SELINUX_ERR` messages are as follows:

- `security_compute_sid`: Invalid context
- `security_validate_transition`: Denied
- `security_bounded_transition`: Denied

Some other messages exist as well, although these are mostly for SELinux-internal problems (related to the SELinux subsystem inside the Linux kernel, such as supported netlink types), which need to be resolved by the SELinux maintainers themselves, and not by policy developers.

Invalid contexts

An invalid context is triggered when a context that is not valid according to the RBAC and SELinux user rules is created. This is usually the case during a domain transition, where the target type is not allowed for the role:

```
time->Wed Aug 4 03:19:04 2014
type=SYSCALL msg=audit(10590262134.246:135): arch=c000003e
  syscall=59
success=no exit=-13 a0=187b190 a1=187b120 a2=187ac30
  a3=7ffff2dc3ec0 items=0
ppid=14696 pid=15085 auid=0 uid=0 gid=0 euid=0 suid=0 fsuid=0
egid=0 sgid=0 fsgid=0 tty=(none) ses=21 comm="logwatch"
  exe="/usr/bin/perl"
subj=system_u:system_r:logwatch_t:s0-s0:c0.c1023 key=(null)
type=SELINUX_ERR msg=audit(10590262134.246:135):
  security_compute_sid:
invalid context system_u:system_r:logwatch_mail_t:s0-s0:c0.c1023 for
scontext=system_u:system_r:logwatch_t:s0-s0:c0.c1023
tcontext=system_u:object_r:sendmail_exec_t:s0 tclass=process
```

Another reason for an invalid context can be that a role transition is triggered, but this role is not allowed for an SELinux user:

```
type=SELINUX_ERR audit(1257378096.775:46): security_compute_sid:
  invalid context
dbadm_u:system_r:mysqld_safe_t:s0 for
  scontext=dbadm_u:dbadm_r:initrc_t:s0
tcontext=system_u:object_r:mysqld_safe_exec_t:s0 tclass=process
```

In both cases, it is important to look at the presented context and the `scontext` and `tcontext` fields. These show the contexts that SELinux finds invalid (presented context) as well as the source (domain initiating the action) and the object context (label through which the new context was decided upon). Based on these, it should be fairly easy to deduce what the error is about.

The first example shows an attempt to transition from the `logwatch_t` domain (which is allowed for the `system_r` role) to the `logwatch_mail_t` domain (which is not allowed for the `system_r` role). To solve this, `logwatch_mail_t` needs to be allowed for the `system_r` role:

```
allow system_r types logwatch_mail_t;
```

The second example is triggered through a role transition. A database administrator launches an `init` script, resulting in the `dbadm_u:dbadm_r:initrc_t` context. This domain executes the `mysqld_safe` application (whose file is labeled `mysqld_safe_exec_t`) that, through the SELinux policy, attempts to perform a role transition to the `system_r` role. Although the `system_r:mysqld_safe_t` context is a valid set, the database administration user itself is not allowed the `system_r` role.

The main issue in this second example is that the context to start from (`dbadm_u:dbadm_r:initrc_t`) shouldn't be used. The `initrc_t` domain should only be allowed for the `system_r` role. This, by itself, requires that the `dbadm_u` SELinux user is also allowed the `system_r` role. So, even though allowing the `system_r` role is the right resolution, the approach taken in the example is wrong (role transition from `initrc_t` to `mysqld_safe_t` instead of role transitioning upon instantiating `initrc_t`).

Denied transition validation

Consider the following error message, which came up when an `init` script tried to increase the sensitivity of a file:

```
type=SELINUX_ERR audit(125482134923.234:25):
  security_validate_transition:
denied for oldcontext=system_u:object_r:selinux_config_t:s0
newcontext=system_u:object_r:selinux_config_t:s15:c0-c1023
taskcontext=system_u:system_r:initrc_t=s0-s16:c0.c1023 tclass=file
```

Such a message occurs when a file transition is performed, but where the target security context is not allowed. SELinux validates whether this is allowed; if not allowed, it logs this through the message.

AVC-like denials will be in place here, but the access vector cache system is only able to validate pair-wise contexts (the source and target contexts), whereas the transition validation needs to be done on three levels (old file context, new file context, and process context).

The solution for the presented error will be to either allow `initrc_t` to raise the security level of a file (through the `mls_file_upgrade` interface) or to not have the `init` script domain try to update the MLS level of a file in the first place.

Denied security-bounded transitions

An example where security-bounded transitions occur is when the `mod_selinux` module is used with Apache (which uses bounded domains and transitions for individual requests). When the target domain is not bounded by the source domain (that is, the SELinux policy does not prevent the target domain from executing an action not allowed by the source domain, as done through the `typebounds` statement), then the following error is displayed:

```
type=SELINUX_ERR msg=audit(1245311998.599:17):
op=security_bounded_transition result=denied
oldcontext=system_u:system_r:httpd_t:s0
newcontext=system_u:system_r:guest_webapp_t:s0
```

When this occurs, a bounded transition is requested by the main application domain (such as when a transition is done for threads), but the target domain is not marked as a bounded domain.

Note that this is different from when a bounded domain is given more privileges—in such cases, SELinux will deny the specific permissions when they are invoked, showing AVC denials.

There's more...

SELinux logging and audit logging is continuously being improved. Work is on the way to make the audit logs easier to parse by scripts and to provide more information. For instance, at the time of writing, a patch has just been accepted to add permissive state information in the AVC logging.

See also

More in-depth analysis and explanation of AVC messages is handled in *SELinux System Administration*, *Packt Publishing*. More resources related to SELinux audit events are available at the following links:

* `http://www.selinuxproject.org/page/NB_AL` (including an overview of all possible fields in AVC events)
* `https://wiki.gentoo.org/wiki/SELinux/Tutorials/Where_to_find_SELinux_permission_denial_details`

Logging positive policy decisions

On some occasions, the system performs actions that the administrator might not expect, but which are allowed by the SELinux policy, making it harder to debug potential problems. An application might be SELinux-aware, causing its own behavior to depend on the SELinux policy, without actually using the SELinux subsystem to enforce access. The SELinux policy might also be configured to behave differently than expected.

In such situations, it might be important to have SELinux log activities that were actually allowed rather than denied; for instance, logging domain transitions to make sure that a transition has indeed occurred.

How to do it...

In order to have domain transitions logged, create an SELinux policy by performing the following steps:

1. Identify the source and target domains to look out for.

2. Create an SELinux policy that calls the `auditallow` statement on the access vector we want to log:

    ```
    auditallow initrc_t postgresql_t:process transition;
    ```

3. Build and load the SELinux policy and try to reproduce the situation.

4. Look at the audit logs and check whether an AVC granted message is displayed:

    ```
    type=AVC msg=audit(1401379369.009:6171): avc:  granted  {
      transition } for pid=4237 comm="rc"
        path="/usr/lib64/postgresql-9.3/bin/pg_ctl" dev="dm-3"
          ino=821490 scontext=system_u:system_r:initrc_t:s0
            tcontext=system_u:system_r:postgresql_t:s0
              tclass=process
    ```

How it works...

Of the many policy statements that SELinux supports, the `auditallow` statement is interesting and does not alter the decisions made by SELinux: having an `auditallow` statement does not allow the action, but rather has the SELinux subsystem log it if it is allowed (through another `allow` statement).

This makes it possible for SELinux policy developers and system administrators to explicitly ask the SELinux subsystem to inform them about decisions taken if the decision is to grant something rather than deny.

Using the `auditallow` statement, we can track SELinux policy decisions and assist in the development of policies and debugging of application behavior, especially when a process is invoked in a very short time frame, as this makes it difficult for administrators to see whether the context of the process is correct (`ps -Z` or by checking the `/proc/<pid>/` contexts).

Some administrators might want to put in some additional logging inside the scripts or commands that they invoke (such as to capture the output of `id -Z`). However, it is very much possible that the SELinux policy does not allow the script to execute the `id` command, let alone show its output or direct its output to a specific logfile.

Enhancing the SELinux policy with additional log types, enabling terminal output, allowing the execution of binaries, and more is quite some overhead just to find out whether the context of the process is as it should be. Using the `auditallow` statement is a great solution to this.

It goes beyond domain transitions, of course. If a file has been changed, and the administrator or engineer is uncertain which process or which context is causing the change, then it is possible to have SELinux audit writes on the file label, as follows:

```
auditallow domain postgresql_etc_t:file write;
```

Thanks to the additional information in the AVC log, we can see which process (PID) running in a particular context (`scontext`) is responsible for writing to the file.

Looking through SELinux constraints

Some denials are caused by SELinux constraints—additional restrictions imposed by the SELinux policy that are not purely based on the SELinux types, but also on the SELinux role and SELinux user. This is often not clear from the denial.

The `audit2why` application helps in informing developers that a denial came from a constraint violation:

```
~# ausearch -m avc -ts recent | grep type=AVC | audit2why
type=AVC msg=audit(1401134596.932:62843): avc:  denied  { search }
  for  pid=19384 comm="mount.nfs4"
    scontext=system_u:system_r:mount_t:s0
      tcontext=system_u:object_r:nfs_t:s0 tclass=dir


        Was caused by:
        Policy constraint violation.


        May require adding a type attribute to the domain or type
        to satisfy the constraint.
```

```
Constraints are defined in the policy sources in
policy/constraints (general), policy/mcs (MCS), and
policy/mls (MLS).
```

This is, however, not always the case, so we need to find a way to investigate whether denials come from constraint violations too.

How to do it...

Although SELinux constraints can be queried easily, they are currently difficult to work with. The following approach helps in validating whether a constraint is applicable for a particular AVC denial that is under investigation:

1. Look through the SELinux policy to see whether the (denied) access has an AVC allow rule or not:

   ```
   ~$ sesearch -s staff_t -t user_home_t -c file -p read -A
   Found 1 semantic av  rules:
     allow staff_t user_home_t : file { … read … };
   ```

2. Assuming there is an allow rule, see whether there are constraints applicable to the operation. This takes into account the class (in the example, this is `file`) and the permission (in the example, this is `read`):

   ```
   ~$ seinfo --constrain | grep 'constrain .* file .* read' -A 1
   ```

3. If constraints might exist, look at the attributes of the source and target contexts, as this is usually how constraints are documented in the policy:

   ```
   ~$ seinfo -tstaff_t -x
   ~$ seinfo -tuser_home_t -x
   ```

4. Inside the SELinux policy, look through the `constraints` file (usually at `${POLICY_LOCATION}/policy/`) and the `mcs` or `mls` file (if the policy uses MCS or MLS), and look for the constraints on the class and permission requested, validating whether there are any expressions concerning the attributes mentioned.

How it works...

Constraints are currently difficult to validate. Luckily, there aren't many constraints in place, but still, not being able to easily verify and look at the constraints is a nuisance for developers.

The complexity increases as the `seinfo --constrain` output, which is the only available method to query constraints next to reading the sources, has the following drawbacks:

- It does not provide any name yet on the constraints (so referring to constraints is difficult)
- It uses **Reverse Polish Notation** (**RPN**), which isn't very user-friendly (although it is powerful for computers, people do not generally read RPN fluently)
- It shows expanded attributes, so we get huge lists of types, rather than a limited set of attributes

The constraint definitions inside the `constraints`, `mcs`, and `mls` files (which are only accessible through the policy source code) are easier to look at. The following example is from the `constraints` file; constraints from `mcs` and `mls` will use the `mlsconstrain` keyword:

```
constrain process { transition dyntransition noatsecure siginh
rlimitinh }
(
..r1 == r2
..or ( t1 == can_change_process_role and t2 == process_user_target )
..or ( t1 == cron_source_domain and t2 == cron_job_domain )
..or ( t1 == can_system_change and r2 == system_r )
..or ( t1 == process_uncond_exempt )
) ;
```

The controls shown use attributes, which are easier to map with a specific situation. It also shows how flexible constraints can be. Next to pure type-oriented rules (`t1` and `t2`), constraints also work with roles (`r1` and `r2`) and can deal with SELinux users (`u1` and `u2`). The number is used to differentiate between the subject (1) and object (2).

As an example, in constraint language, saying that something is allowed if the SELinux users are equal, or the SELinux user of the subject is `system_u`, will be documented as follows:

```
(
    u1 == u2
    or ( u1 == system_u)
)
```

The output of the `seinfo --constrain` command has the advantage that it is easy for computer programs to interpret. Computer programs or scripts, which use the output of `seinfo` to visualize constraint information in a tree-like manner, can be created.

The following GraphViz-generated graph shows the UBAC constraints applicable to file reads, showing only the user domains and the `user_home_t` types (to not overload the graph):

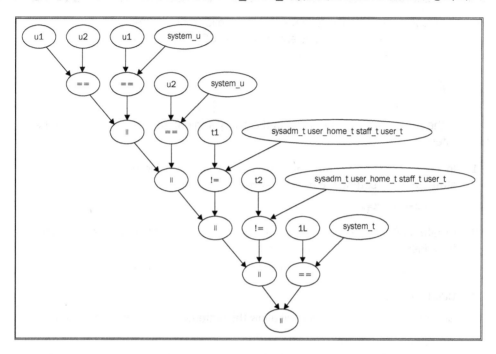

This graph shows how the UBAC constraints are constructed. File reads are prohibited (regardless of the type enforcement rules that are made in the policy), unless they match one of the rules shown in the graph, which are as follows:

- The SELinux user of the subject (domain) and object (resource) are the same
- The SELinux user of the subject is `system_u`
- The SELinux user of the object is `system_u`
- The SELinux type of the subject does not match any of the mentioned types (only a subset is shown in the drawing)
- The SELinux type of the object does not match any of the mentioned types (only a subset is shown in the drawing)
- The SELinux type of the subject is `sysadm_t`

See also

More information on SELinux constraints can be found at the following resources:

- `https://wiki.gentoo.org/wiki/SELinux/Constraints`
- `http://www.selinuxproject.org/page/ConstraintStatements`

Ensuring an SELinux rule is never allowed

It is possible to include statements in the SELinux policy that ensure that a particular access vector cannot be allowed, not even by enhancing the SELinux policy later. This is done with the `neverallow` statement.

How to do it...

To include the `neverallow` statements in the policy and enforce them, go through the following steps:

1. In `/etc/selinux/semanage.conf`, enable support for the `neverallow` statements by setting the `expand-check` variable to 1:

    ```
    expand-check=1
    ```

2. Create an SELinux policy in which the access vectors that should be explicitly forbidden are listed. Consider the following instance:

    ```
    neverallow user_t system_mail_t:process transition;
    ```

3. Build and load the policy.

4. Generate another policy that will allow the statement and attempt to load it:

    ```
    ~$ semodule -i mytest.pp

    libsepol.check_assertion_helper:  neverallow violated by allow
    user_t system_mail_t:process { transition };

    libsemanage.semanage_expand_sandbox: Expand module failed

    semodule: Failed!
    ```

How it works...

Not all distributions enable the assertion checks by default as they incur some performance penalty during policy builds. Some distributions might even have policy incompatibilities due to this, because if the assertions are disabled, then the `neverallow` statements are never processed: the `neverallow` statement isn't really a policy decision, but more a rule that influences loading of new policies, and is enforced by the policy linker (which combines the various policy modules in one final policy binary). As can be deduced from the (failure) output, the `neverallow` statements are implemented as assertions.

Some `neverallow` statements are available as part of the base policy. For instance, the following statement ensures that only the domains with the `selinux_unconfined_type` or `can_load_policy` attribute set can actually load an SELinux policy:

```
neverallow ~{ selinux_unconfined_type can_load_policy }
    security_t:security load_policy;
```

This example uses the negation operator (~), which means *all types except those mentioned*.

Unlike constraints (that can also be used to implement restrictions), the `neverallow` statements help by not accepting any policy that will violate the rule. It is also possible to add the `neverallow` rules through modules, unlike constraints that need to be part of the base SELinux policy (and as such, are governed by Linux distribution, an upstream policy, or developers that manage complete policies rather than individual SELinux policy modules).

The `expand-check` variable in `/etc/selinux/semanage.conf` tells the SELinux user space libraries that the assertion has to be checked. If this variable is set to 0, then the `neverallow` statements have no impact on the policy and its loading whatsoever.

Using strace to clarify permission issues

The `strace` application is a popular debugging application on Linux systems. It allows developers and administrators to look at various system calls made by an application. As SELinux often has access controls on specific system calls, using `strace` can prove to be very useful in debugging permission issues.

How to do it...

To properly use `strace`, follow the next set of steps:

1. Enable the `allow_ptrace` Boolean:

   ```
   ~# setsebool allow_ptrace on
   ```

2. Run the application with `strace`:

   ```
   ~$ strace -o strace.log -f -s 256 tmux
   ```

3. In the resulting logfile, look for the error message that needs to be debugged.

How it works...

The `allow_ptrace` Boolean (on some distributions, the inverse Boolean called `deny_ptrace` is available) needs to be toggled so that the domain that calls `strace` can use `ptrace` (the method that `strace` uses to view system calls) against the target domain. As the `ptrace` method can be a security concern (it allows reading target process' memory, for instance), it is, by default, disabled.

Once an application has been executed through the `strace` application, the logfile will contain all relevant system call information. Of course, on larger applications, or on daemons, this logfile can become massive, so it makes sense to limit the `strace` operation towards a particular subset of system calls, as shown in the following command:

```
~$ strace -e open,access -o strace.log -f -s 256 tmux
```

In this example, only the `open` and `access` system calls are looked at.

In the resulting logfile, the SELinux permission usually issues results in failed system calls with an `EACCES` `(Permission denied)` error code:

```
7313   stat("/", {st_mode=S_IFDIR|0755, st_size=4096, ...}) = 0
7313   stat("/home", {st_mode=S_IFDIR|0755, st_size=4096, ...}) = 0
7313   stat("/home/swift", {st_mode=S_IFDIR|0755, st_size=12288, ...})
= 0
7313   stat("/home/swift/.pki", {st_mode=S_IFDIR|0700, st_size=4096,
...}) = 0
7313   stat("/home/swift/.pki/nssdb", {st_mode=S_IFDIR|0700, st_
size=4096, ...}) = 0
7313   statfs("/home/swift/.pki/nssdb", 0x3c3cab6fa50) = -1 EACCES
(Permission denied)
```

Although an AVC denial will also be shown for most accesses, these denials often do not give a complete picture as to at what stage a denial is in. By using `strace`, we can follow the logic that the application performs.

Sometimes, it isn't obvious why a failure occurs. In this case, it might be interesting to run the application twice—once in enforcing mode and once in permissive mode—and look at the differences in the `strace` logs.

Using strace against daemons

The `strace` application not only makes sense for command-line applications but also for daemons. A popular approach to debugging daemons is to start them from the command line, possibly with a specific debug flag, so that the daemon doesn't detach and run in the background. However, this is often not possible on SELinux: the policy will not allow the daemon to run as a command-line foreground process.

How to do it...

The approach to use `strace` against daemons is similar as with command lines, focusing on the process ID rather than the command:

1. Find out what the process ID of the daemon is:

    `~$ pidof postgres`

    `2557`

2. Use `strace` to attach to the running process:

    `~$ strace -o strace.log -f -s 256 -p 2557`

3. Specify which system calls to watch out for. For instance, permission issues while binding or connecting to ports or sockets can be filtered as follows:

```
~$ strace -e poll,select,connect,recvfrom,sendto -o strace.log -f
-s 256 -p 2557
```

4. Press *Ctrl + C* to interrupt the `strace` session; don't worry, the daemon will continue to run in the background, unharmed.

How it works...

A popular approach to debugging daemons, which is to start the daemon in the foreground from the command line, often does not work on SELinux systems:

```
~$ postgres -D /etc/postgresql-9.3 --data-directory=/srv/pgsql/data
LOG:   could not bind IPv6 socket: Permission denied
WARNING: could not create listen socket for "localhost"
FATAL: could not create any TCP/IP sockets
```

If a user has the rights to execute the daemon binary directly (which isn't default either), then the daemon usually runs with the permissions of the user domain—who hardly has the privileges needed to run the daemon—as there is no transition from the user domain to the daemon domain.

By using `strace` against the daemons, it is possible to debug them in more detail. The `strace` application will bind to the process (using the `ptrace` method) and be notified of every system call that the daemon performs. The `-f` option also ensures that new processes that the daemon launches (for instance, worker processes) are also looked at by `strace`.

To end the `strace` session, it is enough to kill the `strace` session or interrupt it with *Ctrl + C*. The daemon itself is left untouched.

There's more...

Many other system analysis tools, which can be used in a very similar manner, exist. Some examples are SystemTap and Sysdig, with a port of DTrace to Linux being actively developed.

See also

The following resources cover the use of `strace`, SystemTap, and Sysdig in more detail:

- `http://www.dedoimedo.com/computers/strace.html`
- `http://www.thegeekstuff.com/2011/11/strace-examples/`
- `http://www.sourceware.org/systemtap/`
- `http://www.sysdig.org/wiki/`

Auditing system behavior

Another approach to debugging application behavior is through Linux auditing, especially when it is not clear which process is responsible for performing a specific action, as this might make SELinux development a lot more difficult. When developers do not know which domain(s) they need to update privileges for, or do not know how exactly a resource is created, then the Linux audit subsystem can help.

With the Linux auditing subsystem, administrators can enable rules to log activities. In the audit log, the SELinux context of the subject (process) is shown as well, allowing SELinux developers to properly identify the domain to work with.

How to do it...

Let's look at how we can ask the Linux audit subsystem which process is responsible for creating a particular directory in a user's home directory through the following steps:

1. As the root Linux user (and in an SELinux role with sufficient privileges), tell the audit subsystem to log all write- and attribute-changing operations inside the user's home directory:

   ```
   ~# auditctl -w /home/john/ -p wa -k policydev
   ```

2. Perform the necessary action(s) to trigger the behavior that needs to be debugged.

3. Query the audit subsystem for the recent audit events with the `policydev` key:

   ```
   ~# ausearch -ts recent -k policydev
   ```

4. Later, disable the audit rule again so that the audit logs are not cluttered with development-related events:

   ```
   ~# auditctl -W /home/john/ -p wa -k policydev
   ```

How it works...

The Linux audit subsystem uses audit rules to identify which activities need to be logged to the audit log. The rules can be manipulated using the `auditctl` command (audit control).

In our example, a rule was added for the `/home/john/` path (`-w /home/john`) for which the write and attribute changes (`-p wa`) are logged. The events are tagged, so to speak, with a key called `policydev`. Administrators can choose this key freely. Its purpose is to structure audit events and simplify search queries.

When the `auditctl` command is invoked, the rule is immediately active, so after executing the test, audit events will be displayed as follows:

```
time->Sun Jun  8 11:16:47 2014
type=PATH msg=audit(1402219007.623:80705): item=1 name=".dcinforc"
   inode=8364 dev=fd:0c mode=040755 ouid=475395 ogid=475395
      rdev=00:00 obj=user_u:object_r:user_home_t:s0 nametype=CREATE
type=PATH msg=audit(1402219007.623:80705): item=0
   name="/home/john" inode=229 dev=fd:0c mode=040700 ouid=475395
ogid=475395 rdev=00:00 obj=user_u:object_r:user_home_dir_t:s0
      nametype=PARENT
type=CWD msg=audit(1402219007.623:80705):  cwd="/home/john"
type=SYSCALL msg=audit(1402219007.623:80705): arch=c000003e
   syscall=83 success=yes exit=0 a0=7fff33d50330 a1=1ff
      a2=7fff33d50330 a3=a items=2 ppid=23132 pid=23929 auid=475395
         uid=475395 gid=475395 euid=475395 suid=475395 fsuid=475395
            egid=475395 sgid=475395 fsgid=475395 tty=pts3 ses=11203
               comm="java" exe="/usr/bin/java"
                  subj=user_u:user_r:java_t:s0 key="policydev"
```

The logs show that it is a `java` process that is responsible for creating a directory called `.dcinforc/` in the user's home directory. The important fields to consider here are the `nametype=CREATE` (which tells us that an object was created) and `syscall=83` (informing us which system call was trapped by the audit subsystem—in this case, the `mkdir` system call) fields, and of course the `subj=` and `obj=` parameters.

From the example, we can see that there are two distinct `obj=` parameters:

- The first, `obj=user_u:object_r:user_home_t:s0`, is mentioned for the created directory, and it tells us what label the newly created directory received

- The second, `obj=user_u:object_r:user_home_dir_t:s0`, is mentioned for the parent directory (`nametype=PARENT`), informing us what the label of the directory in which `.dcinforc/` is created is

Now, this is just an example of creating directories, but the audit system can trap many types of activities. This is where the `syscall=` field becomes important. This field tells us what specific system call was trapped and logged by the audit subsystem.

A list of system calls and their associated numbers can be found in the proper C header file. For instance, the `/usr/include/asm/unistd_64.h` file (referenced indirectly through `/usr/include/syscalls.h`) contains the following code:

```
#define __NR_rename   82   __SYSCALL(__NR_rename, sys_rename)
#define __NR_mkdir    83   __SYSCALL(__NR_mkdir, sys_mkdir)
#define __NR_rmdir    84   __SYSCALL(__NR_rmdir, sys_rmdir)
```

Through this, we know that the directory was created using the `mkdir` system call and not by any other means (such as creating the directory as a different one first and then renaming it).

There's more...

The audit subsystem receives the rules it needs to follow up on at boot. Most Linux distributions offer a file called `audit.rules` inside `/etc/audit/`, which contains various commands, locations, and system calls that need to be trapped and logged. This file is then read at boot time by the audit daemon `init` script.

If we need to have certain rules loaded automatically—and not just for the duration of a short test—then it is recommended to add the rules to this `audit.rules` script, together with the appropriate comment explaining why this needs to be trapped.

Now, we only used path-based auditing capabilities in the example. The Linux audit subsystem, however, can do much more than just that. For instance, it is possible to audit particular system calls. This allows administrators to keep a close eye on suspicious system call usages, such as the use of `unshare` (which is used for Linux namespaces):

```
~# auditctl -a entry,always -S unshare -k namespace_suspect
```

See also

▸ A good set of default audit rules to work with is mentioned in the CISecurity Benchmark for Red Hat Enterprise Linux, available at `https://benchmarks.cisecurity.org/`

9

Aligning SELinux with DAC

In this chapter, our focus will be on the following set of recipes:

- ▸ Assigning a different root location to regular services
- ▸ Using a different root location for SELinux-aware applications
- ▸ Sharing user content with file ACLs
- ▸ Enabling polyinstantiated directories
- ▸ Configuring capabilities instead of setuid binaries
- ▸ Using group membership for role-based access
- ▸ Backing up and restoring files
- ▸ Governing application network access

Introduction

SELinux is an access control mechanism that works alongside the regular access controls that Linux provides. Making sure that these various access control systems play nicely together is important as both have their merits and uses.

Regular DAC security services on Linux are already quite powerful and are being extended with almost every Linux release. Namespaces, extended access controls, additional **chroot** restrictions, and other services are added to the Linux ecosystem to support the hardening of Linux systems further.

In this process of hardening systems, SELinux is just another layer of defense. Putting all efforts only on SELinux would be a major mistake to make, as SELinux has its downsides as well. By properly enabling the Linux DAC controls and tweaking SELinux so that it plays nicely together with these controls, a Linux system can be made much more resilient against vulnerabilities and attacks.

Assigning a different root location to regular services

A different root location, also known as a chroot, is an important feature of Linux systems meant to disallow direct access to file resources outside a specified directory location. The environment that is accessible from a chroot is called a **jail** or **chroot jail**. Applications in a chroot jail are launched with a different root, wherein only those files that are needed for the application to work are hosted.

Although it is commonly seen as a security feature, this was not the intention of a chroot. However, with the proper approach, chroots can enhance the secure setup of an application.

For instance, in case of a vulnerability, a successful exploit might only be able to access the files available in the chroot. Other sensitive files, such as authentication-related files or other service configurations, are not reachable from within the chroot (assuming the exploited application does not have the privileges to break out of a chroot jail).

The steps to set up a chroot environment for any service are similar, but the end result of a chroot is never the same: different files need to be available in a chroot depending on the application that is being restricted.

Getting ready

Find the application that needs to be restricted. Such applications have to be end services, in the sense that there is little to no interaction between the application and other applications or services. Otherwise, all those other applications and services would need to be available in the same chroot as well.

Usually, the primary targets are those services that are very popular in use on the Internet. Exploits for these services are usually more actively searched and developed for, and when a vulnerability is found and an exploit has been developed, malicious users or groups quickly scan the Internet for vulnerable versions to attack.

How to do it...

The next set of steps shows how to set up a chroot environment and inform SELinux about the chroot. We use the BIND DNS server as our example service and /var/chroot/ as the chroot location:

1. Create the chroot location and add in the necessary subdirectories:

   ```
   ~# mkdir -p /var/chroot/dev
   ~# mkdir -p /var/chroot/etc/bind
   ~# mkdir -p /var/chroot/var/bind/{sec,pri,dyn}
   ~# mkdir -p /var/chroot/var/{log,run}
   ~# chown root:named /var/chroot
   ~# chmod 750 /var/chroot
   ~# chown -R named:named /var/chroot/var/*
   ```

2. Copy all the files that the application needs:

   ```
   ~# cp /etc/named.conf /var/chroot/etc/
   ~# cp /etc/localtime /var/chroot/etc/
   ~# cp -a /var/named/* /var/chroot/var/named/
   ```

3. Create the device files that the application needs:

   ```
   ~# mknod /var/chroot/dev/null c 1 3
   ~# mknod /var/chroot/dev/random c 1 8
   ~# chmod 666 /var/chroot/dev/*
   ```

4. As the BIND service knows about chroots, we do not need to copy its binaries and libraries to the chroot location. However, not all services support chroots out of the box. When this is the case, we need to copy the binaries and libraries as well.

5. Now, relabel the files in the chroot so that they get the proper SELinux labels:

   ```
   ~# setfiles -r /var/chroot/ /etc/selinux/mcs/contexts/files/file_
   contexts /var/chroot/
   ```

6. Launch the application with the proper options to enable the chroot support. Some Linux distributions already support chroot information for the BIND service. In general, it requires the named application to be launched with the -t /var/chroot/ option. If the application does not support chroots out of the box, use the chroot command itself:

   ```
   ~# chroot /var/chroot/ su - named -c /usr/sbin/named
   ```

7. If the application supports chroots out of the box, it might require the chroot capability. This is supported through the sys_chroot permission, granted through the following SELinux policy interface:

```
corecmd_exec_chroot(named_t)
```

How it works...

Setting up a chroot environment is usually a trial-and-error approach; although, for more popular services, many tutorials exist on the Internet that make setting up chroots a lot easier.

The basic approach to use is four-fold:

1. Create the chroot location and directory structure.
2. Install the necessary files and, if necessary, application binaries and libraries.
3. Update the SELinux labels of the resources.
4. Call the chroot binary or use the built-in chroot capabilities of the application.

When creating a chroot location, we need to make sure that the structure is similar to a real root location (that is, the / location); as for the application, it will see the filesystem as if this chroot location is the entire filesystem.

Which files to install is a different matter though, and having online resources to inform us what to do is a great help. But if these online resources are missing, then we can still find out which files are needed.

For instance, we can use the ldd or scanelf application:

```
~# ldd /usr/sbin/named
  linux-vdso.so.1
  liblwres.so.90 => /usr/lib64/liblwres.so.90
  libdns.so.100 => /usr/lib64/libdns.so.100
  libbind9.so.90 => /usr/lib64/libbind9.so.90
  libisccfg.so.90 => /usr/lib64/libisccfg.so.90
  libisccc.so.90 => /usr/lib64/libisccc.so.90
  libisc.so.95 => /usr/lib64/libisc.so.95
  libc.so.6 => /lib64/libc.so.6
  /lib64/ld-linux-x86-64.so.2
```

But in general, it is the trial-and-error approach that works the easiest. Just launch the application in the chroot, register its errors, and resolve them.

For SELinux, the important bit here is that the chroot should be labeled correctly. Consider `/var/chroot/etc/named.conf`, for instance. The SELinux policy will assume that this file is labeled `named_conf_t`. However, the location itself (`/var/chroot/etc/named.conf`) implies `var_t`, as `/var/` is `var_t` and there are no definitions for any of our defined location's subdirectories or files within.

The `setfiles` command allows us to relabel a location with a different root location, resulting in `/var/chroot/etc/named.conf` being labeled as if it was `/etc/named.conf`. However, take care that a system relabeling operation is followed by the `setfiles` command again as the SELinux configuration is not aware of this change in labeling.

Finally, the application itself needs to be launched inside the chroot or through its built-in chroot support. Applications that support chroots themselves can be tuned through their configuration files and start up options to make sure that they run in a chroot environment. If that isn't possible, then the application should be started using an `init` script that calls the `chroot` command, most likely together with the `su` application to allow switching to a different user.

There's more...

A chroot is a relatively primitive yet powerful method for reducing the impact of an exploit. However, methods exist to escape a chroot. Luckily, there are some kernel patches that improve the security of chroots tremendously. A popular update is the one maintained by the **grsecurity** team (`http://www.grsecurity.net`).

With grsecurity's chroot restrictions, the kernel can be configured with the following options:

- Disallow mounts and remounts of filesystems initiated from within the chroot
- Disallow chrooting from within the chroot
- Disallow the `pivot_root` call from within the chroot
- Force the current working directory of chrooted applications to be the root directory of the chroot
- Disallow the `setuid` and `setgid chmod` operations from within the chroot
- Disallow changing directories through open file descriptors pointing outside the chroot
- Disallow attaching to shared memory created outside the chroot
- Disallow access to Unix domain sockets created outside the chroot
- Disallow sending signals to processes outside the chroot

Besides these options, there are many, many more options. Such options make chroot jails much more security-oriented than originally intended and make for a very powerful mitigation against exploits.

See also

There are many resources available about chroot jails and BIND chroots in particular:

▸ Building and configuring BIND 9 in a chroot jail available at `http://www.unixwiz.net/techtips/bind9-chroot.html` goes in great detail and has pointers to various other BIND-related resources

▸ On the same site, best practices for Unix `chroot()` operations can be found: `http://www.unixwiz.net/techtips/chroot-practices.html`

▸ The Jailkit project (`http://olivier.sessink.nl/jailkit/`) provides a set of utilities to manage chroot jails

Using a different root location for SELinux-aware applications

SELinux-aware applications have more requirements when they run inside a chroot location. They require access to the SELinux subsystem (from within the chroot) and possibly SELinux configuration entries. This includes PAM-enabled services, as user logins on these services might require access to the SELinux user configuration files (such as the `seusers` file and default contexts).

How to do it...

First, create the regular chroot location as we saw earlier. To update the system to support SELinux-aware applications inside the chroot, complete the following steps:

1. Mount the SELinux filesystem inside the chroot at `/sys/fs/selinux/` so that the application can query the SELinux policy:

   ```
   ~# mkdir -p /var/chroot/sys/fs/selinux
   ~# mount -t selinuxfs none /var/chroot/sys/fs/selinux
   ```

2. Optionally, create the `/var/chroot/etc/selinux/` location and copy the current definition inside it:

   ```
   ~# cp -a /etc/selinux/ /var/chroot/etc/
   ```

3. Update the `seusers` file (in `/var/chroot/etc/selinux/mcs/`) to only contain the SELinux user mapping(s) needed inside the chroot.

How it works...

Applications that are SELinux-aware usually require access to the SELinux filesystem (`/sys/fs/selinux/`) and a kernel-provided pseudo filesystem needed in order to interact with the SELinux subsystem. This should be seen as a more dangerous situation, as this usually has the application run as a more privileged user and with access to a system resource that is not protected by the chroot anymore. This reduces the effectiveness of a chroot jail as a security measure.

If applications do not support chroots themselves internally, then we will have to expose the `/sys/fs/selinux/` filesystems to the application that is chrooted. If the application supports chroot out of the box, it might only call the chroot after consulting SELinux (that is, from the nonchrooted parent) and run the worker or user processes inside a chroot. This is the case with chrooted SFTP users supported through OpenSSH.

It might also be sufficient to mount the SELinux filesystem on `/selinux/` (a deprecated but still a supported location for the SELinux filesystem) inside the chroot. That way, no fake `/sys/fs/` location needs to be created:

```
~# mount -t selinuxfs none /var/chroot/selinux
```

The `/etc/selinux/` location is not always needed, so it shouldn't be made accessible inside the chroot by default. SELinux-aware applications that use SELinux user and role transitions or that actively modify file contexts will need to be able to read the files inside `/etc/selinux/` though.

Depending on the reason of the chroot jail, it might be possible as well to use a read-only bind-mount of the `/etc/selinux/` location:

```
~# mount -o bind /etc/selinux /var/chroot/etc/selinux
~# mount -o remount,ro /var/chroot/etc/selinux
```

The remount afterwards is needed to mark it as read-only. A bind-mount, by itself, doesn't allow additional mount options to be passed, so we cannot immediately mount with the `ro` mount option. Of course, it is no longer possible/needed to modify the `seusers` file with a read-only bind-mount.

See also

► Detailed guides on SFTP chroots can be found at `https://wiki.archlinux.org/index.php/SFTP_chroot` and `http://en.wikibooks.org/wiki/OpenSSH/Cookbook/SFTP`

Sharing user content with file ACLs

Access control lists allow for more fine-grained access controls on files. Instead of using a common group ownership, access to files can be individually granted to users or groups.

However, the access controls that SELinux enables should also be tailored to this situation. Features such as the user-based access control constraints in SELinux might prevent sharing user content altogether, regardless of the ACLs set on the file.

How to do it...

Assuming that a user wants to allow read and read-write accesses to a set of files and directories, the following set of steps can be used:

1. Create an accessible location outside the user's home directory:

   ```
   ~# mkdir -p /home/share/
   ~# chmod 1777 /home/share/
   ```

2. Create an SELinux file type that can be used for sharing resources:

   ```
   type user_share_t;
   files_type(user_share_t)
   ```

3. Create an interface allowing users to administer the resource:

   ```
   interface(`userdom_admin_user_share','
     gen_require(`
       type user_share_t;
     ')
     admin_pattern($1, user_share_t)
   ')
   ```

4. Assign this type to the new location:

   ```
   ~# semanage fcontext -a -t user_share_t "/home/share(/.*)?"
   ~# restorecon -R /home/share/
   ```

5. Assign the interface to the user domain(s) that will participate in the shared development of this resource:

   ```
   userdom_admin_user_share(user_t)
   ```

6. Move the files that need to be shared outside the user's home directory, as the SELinux context of the home directory will not allow sharing resources within.

   ```
   ~$ cp -r sharedfiles/ /home/share && rm -r sharedfiles/
   ```

7. Assign the ACL that allows the (limited set of) users proper access:

```
~$ setfacl -R -m u:user1:rX /home/share/sharedfiles
~$ setfacl -R -m u:user2:rwX /home/share/sharedfiles
~$ setfacl -m "default:u:user2:rwX" /home/share/sharedfiles
~$ setfacl -m "default:u:user0:rwX" /home/share/sharedfiles
~$ setfacl -m "default:u:user1:rX" /home/share/sharedfiles
```

How it works...

The file-level access controls can be perfectly used together with the SELinux access controls. However, special care needs to be taken that both control mechanisms (file ACLs and the SELinux policy) don't interfere with each other. SELinux might disallow accesses expected to work (for instance, due to SELinux constraints rather than type enforcement settings), but also file access controls need to be properly managed in order to keep the behavior on the system consistent.

In the recipes, the files that are shared are moved outside the user's home directory. This is mostly because of SELinux' UBAC feature, which disallows different SELinux users to access each others' regular resources (such as those labeled as user_home_t but also user_home_dir_t). As user_home_dir_t isn't accessible by other SELinux users under the UBAC constraints, users mapped to a different SELinux user will not be able to enter and search through the sharing user's home directory, regardless of ACLs being installed.

Not all systems have UBAC enabled, or the sharing might be within a single SELinux user, so this approach is not always necessary. Still, using a different location allows for better management. Consider the case where the first user exits the company, but his team wants to continue accessing and managing the shared resources. They would disappear if the user home directory is removed.

With the files moved to a different location, the next step is to label the files with a file type that all users can access, but which isn't restricted by the UBAC feature. File types that have the ubac_constrained_type attribute set cannot be used for sharing, so a new file type is created that is labeled as a regular file. The user domains are then granted administrative rights on this type (allowing them not only to manage the files, but also to relabel files to or from the user_share_t type). This ensures that SELinux doesn't prevent access to the shared resources, while still preventing unauthorized domains to access the resources.

It might also be sufficient to pick a file type that is already accessible by users, such as the nfs_t type (if the SELinux Boolean, use_nfs_home_dirs, is set). However, assigning a type that is functionally used for different reasons (nfs_t is for NFS-mounted filesystems) might open up access to these resources from other domains as well. As such, administrators need to carefully consider the reasons for and the consequences of each choice.

After labeling the `/home/share/` location with the `user_share_t` type, the original user copies the resources to the new location and removes them from the current one. This approach (copy and remove) is used to ensure that resources inherit the label of the target location (`user_share_t`) instead of keeping the labels associated with the original file location (`user_home_t`), as would be the case with a move (`mv`) command. In more recent `coreutils` packages, support for `mv -Z` is made available, which allows you to move the resources directly while still giving the resources a proper context.

A third approach for the user would be to move the resources first and then relabel them:

```
~$ mv sharedfiles/ /home/share/
~$ chcon -R -t user_share_t /home/share/sharedfiles/
```

Finally, with all SELinux rules and support in place, the file access controls are enabled on the shared resources, and a default ACL is enabled so that write operations by other users will automatically inherit the proper ACL on the written resource as well, making sure that all users cooperating on the shared resource don't need to continuously set ACLs on the files.

Without the default ACLs, other users might create files inside `sharedfiles/` that have no ACLs set, disallowing other users to access the resources.

There's more...

Another approach that could be taken is to use the `setgid` group ownership. For instance, if all users that participate in the shared files access are in a `shrgrp` group, then the following will automatically have all files created inside the mentioned directory have the `shrgrp` group ownership defined as well:

```
~$ chgrp -R shrgrp /home/share/sharedfiles/
~$ find /home/share/sharedfiles/ -type d -exec chmod g+s '{}' \;
```

This does require the users to have a proper `umask` setting (such as `007` or less) so that the group permission on the newly created resource allows read and write accesses for group members.

Enabling polyinstantiated directories

On Linux and Unix systems, the `/tmp/` and `/var/tmp/` locations are world writable. They are used to provide a common location for temporary files and are protected through the sticky bit so that users cannot remove files they don't own from the directory, even though the directory is world writable.

But despite this measure, there is a history of attacks against the `/tmp/` and `/var/tmp/` locations, such as race conditions with symbolic links and information leakage through (temporary or not) world or group-readable files generated within.

Polyinstantiated directories provide a neat solution to this problem: users get their own, private /tmp/ and /var/tmp/ instance. These directory instances are created upon login on a different location, but then made visible (mounted) on the /tmp/ and /var/tmp/ locations for that specific user session. This mount is local to the user session through the use of Linux namespaces—other users have their own view on the mounts, and for administrators, polyinstantiation is not enabled, so they keep a global view on the system.

How to do it...

To enable polyinstantiation of /tmp/ and /var/tmp/, the following steps should be followed:

1. Create the /tmp-inst/ and /var/tmp/tmp-inst/ locations:

   ```
   ~# mkdir /tmp-inst/ /var/tmp/tmp-inst/
   ~# chmod 000 /tmp-inst/ /var/tmp/tmp-inst/
   ```

2. Set the label for these locations as tmp_t:

   ```
   ~# semanage fcontext -a -t tmp_t -f d /tmp-inst
   ~# semanage fcontext -a -t tmp_t -f d /var/tmp/tmp-inst
   ```

3. Edit /etc/security/namespace.conf and add in the following definitions:

   ```
   /tmp      /tmp-inst/      level   root,adm
   /var/tmp  /var/tmp/tmp-inst/   level   root,adm
   ```

4. Edit the PAM configuration file used by logins, such as system-login, and add the following line to the session group after the pam_selinux.so one:

   ```
   session   required   pam_namespace.so
   ```

5. Enable the allow_polyinstantiation SELinux Boolean:

   ```
   ~# setsebool -P allow_polyinstantiation on
   ```

How it works...

The system preparation for polyinstantiated directories requires that the directories themselves are available and have the proper permissions set. When the parent directory, such as /tmp/, is a tmpfs mount, then we cannot have the polyinstantiated directories made available inside of it (such as /tmp/tmp-inst/), as that directory would be missing after a reboot (unless it is added through the init scripts); hence the setup of /tmp-inst/ as a separate location. Of course, administrators can still opt to have this location itself as a tmpfs mount—the important thing is that the directory must exist and have the proper permissions (which is represented by the 000 permission set).

In the example, /var/tmp/ is assumed not to be a tmpfs mount, so we can define the polyinstantiated directories inside of it.

The configuration file for polyinstantiated directories is the `namespace.conf` file under `/etc/security/`. In it, the mount-point is mentioned together with the directory in which the polyinstantiated directories are created:

```
/tmp   /tmp-inst/   level   root,adm
```

The third column defines the method for polyinstantiation. On non-SELinux systems, the most common method used is the `user` method, which creates directories based on the username. On SELinux-enabled systems, the method must be either `level` or `context`.

In case of the `level` method, the directories are created based on the username and MLS level of the user session. The `context` method has directories created based on the username and security context. This allows for hiding temporary data based on the role of the user, so accidental data leakage is less likely to occur.

Administrators can access the polyinstantiated directories as they are excluded from the polyinstantiation: the excluded list of users is configured as the fourth column in the `namespace.conf` file. Administrators can still see the directories that are created dynamically:

```
~# ls -l /tmp-inst/
drwxrwxrwt. 2 root root 4096 Jun 22 12:31
system_u:object_r:tmp_t:s0_user1
drwxrwxrwt. 2 root root 4096 Jun 22 12:30
system_u:object_r:tmp_t:s0_user2
```

Next, the PAM configuration file(s) are modified to enable the `pam_namespace.so` library. To find the PAM configuration files that need to be edited, look for the PAM configuration files that call `pam_selinux.so`:

```
~# cd /etc/pam.d
~# grep -l pam_selinux.so *
system-login
```

In this example, the `system-login` PAM configuration file is the only file calling `pam_selinux.so`, so the `pam_namespace.so` line is added to this file. The line must be added after the `pam_selinux.so` call as the `pam_namespace.so` file uses the context of the user to decide how to call the instantiated directory. If `pam_selinux.so` has not been called yet, then this information is not available and the logon will fail.

Finally, the SELinux Boolean, `allow_polyinstantiation`, is enabled so that the proper domains have the privilege to create (and change the contexts of) the proper directories, to use namespaces, to check user context, and more.

There's more...

Administrators can go further than just having the directories created when needed. During the setup of polyinstantiated directories, a script called `namespace.init`, which is available at `/etc/security/` is called to further handle the creation and modification of those directories.

This script can be adjusted to copy files towards the instantiated directory (the file usually contains this logic already for polyinstantiated home directories) or do other changes, allowing to further tune the setup for a user session.

The `systemd init` system also has support for polyinstantiated `/tmp/` directories through the `PrivateTmp` directive, which provides a private `/tmp/` directory for a service rather than end users.

Configuring capabilities instead of setuid binaries

Linux capabilities allow for course-grained kernel security authorizations on the user and application levels. Before capabilities existed, administrators could only grant additional privileges to users through `setuid` applications: applications which, when executed, inherit the privileges of the owner of the application (usually, `root`). With capabilities, the set of privileges can be restricted further.

For instance, the `ping` application can be granted the `cap_net_raw` capability, so it does not need to be `setuid` anymore. Depending on the setup, either users need to be granted the possible use of the capability (if the application has the proper flag set) or the capability is granted immediately (regardless of user settings).

How to do it...

To use capabilities with SELinux, execute the following steps:

1. Enable the capabilities that are needed for an application on the application binary:

    ```
    ~# setcap cap_net_raw+ei /bin/ping
    ```

2. For the users that are allowed to use the `net_raw` capability, add the proper configurations in `/etc/security/capability.conf` (one line per user):

    ```
    cap_net_raw    user1
    ```

3. SELinux domains that will use the capability need to be granted the use of it. For common applications, this is usually already in place.

    ```
    allow ping_t self:capability net_raw;
    ```

4. SELinux domains that are allowed to modify the capability set assigned to their process(es) must have the `setcap` privilege set:

```
allow local_login_t self:process setcap;
```

5. Edit the PAM configuration file(s) for the services through which the capabilities are allowed, and add the following line to the `auth` configuration block:

```
auth  required  pam_cap.so
```

6. If capabilities need to be tracked/audited, SELinux's `auditallow` statement can be used:

```
auditallow domain self:capability net_raw;
```

How it works...

The capabilities that a process is currently allowed to use are called the permitted capabilities. The capabilities that are active are the effective capabilities. A third set of capabilities are inheritable capabilities.

In the example, we enabled the `cap_net_raw` capability for the `ping` application and marked the capability as effective if it is inherited. In other words, it is not enabled (permitted) by default. If we want to enable the `cap_net_raw` capability immediately, we would use the effective and permitted set:

```
~# setcap cap_net_raw+ep /bin/ping
```

Applications that are capability-aware do not need to have the `effective` bit set. They will enable (and drop) the capabilities as they are needed through the proper system calls (which is why the `setcap` permission is needed for these domains). If `ping` was capability-aware, then the following would be sufficient for our example:

```
~# setcap cap_net_raw+i /bin/ping
```

Next, the users that are allowed the `cap_net_raw` capability (through the selected set of applications) need to be granted the `cap_net_raw` capability in their inherited capability set. This is done through the `capability.conf` file in `/etc/security/` and by calling the `pam_cap.so` module from within the proper PAM configuration files. The use of PAM configuration files also allows us to differentiate capabilities based on the service through which a user logs on.

To check the currently enabled capabilities, users can execute the `capsh` application:

```
~$ /sbin/capsh --print | grep ^Current
Current: cap_net_raw+i
```

To see the capabilities on a file, the `getcap` application can be used:

```
~$ getcap /bin/ping
/bin/ping = cap_net_raw+ei
```

Finally, auditing the use of capabilities through the `auditallow` statement tells us when (and by whom) a capability was used, although the same can be accomplished without an SELinux policy using the Linux audit subsystem, auditing for the `setcap` system call.

See also

▶ Capabilities are well explained in Chris Friedhoff's **POSIX Capabilities & File POSIX Capabilities** page (`http://www.friedhoff.org/posixfilecaps.html`)

Using group membership for role-based access

In larger environments, access controls are usually granted based on group membership. Group membership is easier to manage than individual permissions: just adding or removing users from a group automatically grants or revokes permissions, and administrators can easily find out which permission(s) a user will have based on the group membership.

How to do it...

In order to use group membership as a high-level method for assigning permissions, administrators need to take care of the following aspects:

1. Add user(s) to the groups they should belong to:

   ```
   ~# gpasswd -a user1 dba
   ~# gpasswd -a user1 dev
   ```

2. Assign the proper SELinux user to the group:

   ```
   ~# semanage login -s dbadm_u %dba
   ```

3. Restrict binaries and libraries that should only be called by a specific group:

   ```
   ~# chgrp -R dev /usr/lib/gcc /usr/x86_64-pc-linux-gnu/gcc-bin
   ~# chmod -R o-rx /usr/lib/gcc /usr/x86_64-pc-linux-gnu/gcc-bin
   ```

4. Use group notation inside the `sudoers` file to grant specific privileges to group members:

   ```
   %dba  ALL=(ALL)  TYPE=dbadm_t ROLE=dbadm_r NOPASSWD: initdb
   ```

How it works...

Using groups makes permission handling much easier. In the end, this allows administrators to just handle group membership for users and automatically assign privileges based on the groups.

We can grant groups an SELinux user, and through the group membership decide which SELinux user a regular user is logged into. Of course, users can belong to multiple groups. For SELinux, it is the order of the `seusers` file that decides which of the following mappings are used:

- ▶ SELinux user mappings for individual users take precedence over group mappings
- ▶ The first group mapping in the `seusers` file that uses a group that the Linux user is a member of decides the SELinux user mapping if no individual SELinux user mappings exist for this user

As such, if a user is a member of two groups (say, `dba` and `web`) and there are mappings to both `dbadm_u` (for the `dba` group) and `webadm_u` (for the `web` group), then the first mapping in the `seusers` file will decide what the user's SELinux user will be.

In order to override this, either add the user individually or create another group (say, `dbaweb`), grant the user this group as well, and put that group mapping at the beginning of the list in the `seusers` file.

When only a specific user group is allowed access to an application, but that application does not use any specific SELinux domains, then it might be more flexible for administrators to use the Linux DAC permissions to restrict access to the application. By only allowing a specific group (`dev`, in our example), read and execute rights on the application and application libraries, we can restrict access easily.

Another approach is to label the files with new SELinux types and grant the proper domains access to those types. However, this might lead to a large set of domains needing access to the types (and so requires massive policy development effort), whereas the Linux DAC approach is easily implemented.

Backing up and restoring files

An important aspect to the availability of a system and the security of a service is to provide backup and restore services. For many, having a copy of the files available might seem sufficient as a backup approach. However, backups should contain more than just the content of a file.

How to do it...

When selecting a backup solution, make sure to check for the following:

1. A selection of the extended attributes of the files should be backed up as well (and not only the `security.selinux` one).

2. When files are restored onto their original location, the SELinux context should be restored with it as well. If the backup solution doesn't support SELinux contexts, the `restorecon` command should be invoked afterwards against the restored file(s).

3. When files are restored into a temporary area, the SELinux context should not be restored. Instead, the administrator should put the file back in place and restore the context afterwards.

4. The SELinux configuration in `/etc/selinux/` should definitely be backed up, even if no full system backups are used. Whenever the policy or file context definitions are altered, these should be backed up as well whenever files are backed up.

How it works...

File labels are stored as the `security.selinux` extended attribute. As the functioning of a policy is based on the labels of all objects involved, not backing up and restoring the file labels might jeopardize the functioning of the system after a restore operation.

When the backup solution does not support extended attributes, it is important that all labels are properly set through the `semanage fcontext` command. This is the only way to make sure that, after a restore, the admin can run `restorecon` against the restored files in order to reset the file labels:

```
~# tar xvf /path/to/last_backup.tar.gz etc/named.conf
~# restorecon /etc/named.conf
```

However, it is seriously recommended to select a backup solution that supports extended attributes as many other Linux-related settings are stored as extended attributes. The file ACLs, for instance, are stored as extended attributes as well:

```
~$ getfattr -m . -d named.conf
# file: named.conf
security.selinux="system_u:object_r:named_conf_t:s0"
system.posix_acl_access=0sAgAAAAEABgD/////AgAGAOo...
```

Other examples of extended attributes that can be used on a system are PaX markings (`user.pax.flags`), IMA and EVM hashes (`security.ima` and `security.evm`), and capabilities (`security.capability`). But herein lies the problem as well: some attributes shouldn't (or cannot) be restored. The IMA and EVM attributes, for instance, are handled by the Linux kernel and cannot be manipulated by user utilities.

Alongside the file labels, backing up and restoring the SELinux policy should be integrated as well, especially on a system with a modified SELinux policy. If a policy is different after a restore, then types might be missing and labels might become invalid.

Governing application network access

On Linux systems, `iptables` (and more recently, `nftables`) is the de facto host-based firewall technology. Administrators will undoubtedly use it to prevent access to a service from unauthorized systems. We can also use `iptables` to identify and label network packets, allowing only authorized applications (domains) to send or receive those network packets.

By default, the SELinux policy supports client and server packets and allows the usual domains access to their client and/or server packets. For instance, the web server domains (such as `httpd_t`) will have the privileges to send and receive `http_server_packet_t` packets:

```
allow httpd_t http_server_packet_t:packet { send recv };
```

This is provided through the `corenet_sendrecv_http_server_packets` interface. Enabling packet labeling is simply done using `iptables` as will be shown through this recipe. But to properly govern network access, custom packet types will need to be created to ensure that no default allowed access is used.

How to do it...

To only allow authorized domains access to particular network packets (datagrams and data streams), use the following approach:

1. Identify the flow that needs to be allowed. For instance, we might only want DNS requests from `10.11.12.0/24` to be accepted by the `dnsmasq_t` domain, and requests from `10.13.14.0/24` to be accepted by the `named_t` domain.

2. Create two new packet types:
   ```
   type dnsmasq_server_packet_t;
   corenet_server_packet(dnsmasq_server_packet_t)

   type named_server_packet_t;
   corenet_server_packet(named_server_packet_t)
   ```

3. Allow the domains send and receive privileges for these packets:
   ```
   allow dnsmasq_t dnsmasq_server_packet_t:packet { send recv };
   allow named_t named_server_packet_t:packet { send recv };
   ```

4. Label the incoming traffic accordingly:

```
~# iptables -t mangle -A INPUT -p tcp -s 10.11.12.0/24 --dport
   53 -j SECMARK --selctx
     "system_u:object_r:dnsmasq_server_packet_t:s0"
~# iptables -t mangle -A INPUT -p udp  -s 10.11.12.0/24
   --dport 53 -j SECMARK --selctx
     "system_u:object_r:dnsmasq_server_packet_t:s0"
~# iptables -t mangle -A INPUT -p tcp -s 10.13.14.0/24 --dport
   53 -j SECMARK --selctx
     "system_u:object_r:named_server_packet_t:s0"
~# iptables -t mangle -A INPUT -p udp -s 10.13.14.0/24 --dport
   53 -j SECMARK --selctx
     "system_u:object_r:named_server_packet_t:s0"
```

How it works...

By using custom network packet labels, access from or to specific applications can be governed using an SELinux policy. Even though multiple applications can accept incoming DNS requests, this recipe shows how to ensure that only one application can deal with requests that have passed a certain filter.

Whenever a SECMARK label is enabled with `iptables`, the Linux kernel will automatically enable SECMARK labeling on all packets. Packets that are not marked specifically by the administrator will be marked with the `unlabeled_t` type. Some domains are allowed to handle the `unlabeled_t` packets through the `corenet_sendrecv_unlabeled_packets` interface (or the `kernel_sendrecv_unlabeled_packets` interface). However, if that is not the case, then those domains will not be able to handle network traffic anymore.

As such, it is advised to use the standard labeling for other incoming (and outgoing) traffic. To identify which incoming traffic should be labeled, we can leverage assistance from the `netstat` output:

```
~# netstat -naptZ | awk '/LISTEN/ {print $4,$6,$7,$8}'
0.0.0.0:13500 LISTEN 6489/mysqld system_u:system_r:mysqld_t:s0
0.0.0.0:80 LISTEN 23303/httpd system_u:system_r:httpd_t:s0
10.11.12.122:53 LISTEN 4432/dnsmasq system_u:system_r:dnsmasq_t:s0
10.13.14.42:53 LISTEN 5423/named system_u:system_r:named_t:s0
```

Based on this output, labeling the appropriate traffic as `mysqld_server_packet_t` and `http_server_packet_t` will allow those domains to access their incoming network traffic.

By creating additional types for `dnsmasq_t` and `named_t`, those applications can only handle requests associated with those packet types. If an administrator changes the configuration of one of these DNS servers, then the network packet labeling will still ensure that DNS requests from the previously identified network segments cannot be used by the wrong DNS server, even though the flow is allowed firewall-wise.

With `sesearch`, interrogating the policy to see which applications (domains) are able to send and receive certain packets is easy:

```
~# sesearch -t dns_server_packet_t -ACTS
Found 10 semantic av rules:
    allow nova_network_t dns_server_packet_t : packet { send recv } ;
    allow corenet_unconfined_type packet_type : packet { send recv
relabelto flow_in flow_out forward_in forward_out } ;
    allow named_t dns_server_packet_t : packet { send recv } ;
    allow vmware_host_t server_packet_type : packet { send recv } ;
    allow dnsmasq_t dns_server_packet_t : packet { send recv } ;
    allow kernel_t packet_type : packet send ;
    allow iptables_t packet_type : packet relabelto ;
ET allow squid_t packet_type : packet { send recv } ;
[ squid_connect_any ]
DT allow icecast_t packet_type : packet { send recv } ;
[ icecast_connect_any ]
DT allow git_session_t server_packet_type : packet { send recv } ;
[ git_session_bind_all_unreserved_ports ]
```

The same approach can be taken from a client level. A mail server might need to connect to other mail servers, which means that the outgoing data can be labeled as `mail_client_packet_t` (if we use the default traffic). However, if we want to make sure only the mail server can connect to other mail servers (and no other domains that also have privileges to send and receive the `mail_client_packet_t` packets), then a new packet type can be used.

See also

For more information about SECMARK labeling, read up on the following resources:

  ▶ `http://www.selinuxproject.org/page/NB_Networking`
  ▶ Paul Moore's **Transitioning to Secmark** at `http://paulmoore.livejournal.com/4281.html`
  ▶ James Morris's **New Secmark-based network controls for SELinux** at `http://james-morris.livejournal.com/11010.html`

10
Handling SELinux-aware Applications

In this chapter, we will cover handling of SELinux-aware applications through the following recipes:

- ▶ Controlling D-Bus message flows
- ▶ Restricting service ownership
- ▶ Understanding udev's SELinux integration
- ▶ Using cron with SELinux
- ▶ Checking the SELinux state programmatically
- ▶ Querying SELinux userland configuration in C
- ▶ Interrogating the SELinux subsystem code-wise
- ▶ Running new processes in a new context
- ▶ Reading the context of a resource

Introduction

For most applications, the SELinux subsystem in the Linux kernel is capable of enforcing security controls without further interaction with other applications and components. However, there are actions that cannot be handled by the SELinux subsystem autonomously. Some applications execute commands for specific users, but the target domain cannot be deduced from the path of the application that is itself being executed, making type transitions based on the label impossible.

One solution for this problem is to make the application SELinux-aware, having the application interrogate the SELinux subsystem as to what should be the context of the newly executed application. Once the context is obtained, the application can then instruct the SELinux subsystem that this context can be assigned to the process that will be launched next.

Of course, it isn't only about deciding what context a process should be in. Applications can also check the SELinux policy and act on the policy themselves, rather than having the policies enforced through the Linux kernel. If applications use SELinux to get more information about a session and set contexts based on this information, then we call these applications SELinux-aware.

The easiest method to see whether an application is SELinux-aware is to check the documentation, or to check whether it is linked with the `libselinux.so` library:

```
~$  ldd /usr/sbin/crond | grep selinux
  libselinux.so.1 => /lib64/libselinux.so.1 (0x00007fa53299a000)
```

Some SELinux-aware applications not only query information, but also enforce decisions on objects that the SELinux subsystem in the Linux kernel cannot control. Examples of such objects are the database objects in the **Security Enhanced PostgreSQL** (**SEPostgreSQL**) application or the D-Bus services. Although represented in the SELinux policy, they are not part of the regular Linux operating system but are instead owned by the application itself. Such SELinux-aware applications are called **user space object managers**.

Regardless of how an application handles its SELinux-specific code, whenever such applications are used on a system, it is important to know how the SELinux code in the application works, as the standard approach (look at AVC denials and see whether a context needs to be changed or the policy tuned) might not work at all in these cases.

Controlling D-Bus message flows

D-Bus implementation on Linux is an example of an SELinux-aware application, acting as a user space object manager. Applications can register themselves on a bus and can send messages between applications through D-Bus. These messages can be controlled through the SELinux policy as well.

Getting ready

Before looking at the SELinux access controls related to message flows, it is important to focus on a D-Bus service and see how its authentication is done (and how messages are relayed in D-Bus) as this is reflected in the SELinux integration.

Go to `/etc/dbus-1/system.d/` (which hosts the configuration files for D-Bus services) and take a look at a configuration file. For instance, the service configuration file for `dnsmasq` looks like the following:

```
<!DOCTYPE busconfig PUBLIC "-//freedesktop//DTD D-BUS Bus
   Configuration 1.0//EN" "http://www.freedesktop.org/standards/
dbus/1.0/busconfig.dtd">
<busconfig>
  <policy user="root">
    <allow own="uk.org.thekelleys.dnsmasq"/>
    <allow send_destination="uk.org.thekelleys.dnsmasq"/>
  </policy>
  <policy context="default">
    <deny own="uk.org.thekelleys.dnsmasq"/>
    <deny send_destination="uk.org.thekelleys.dnsmasq"/>
  </policy>
</busconfig>
```

This configuration tells D-Bus that only the root Linux user is allowed to have a service *own* the `uk.org.thekelleys.dnsmasq` service and send messages to this service. Others (as managed through the default policy) are denied these operations.

On a system with SELinux enabled, having root as the finest granularity doesn't cut it. So, let's look at how the SELinux policy can offer a fine-grained access control in D-Bus.

How to do it...

To control D-Bus message flows with SELinux, perform the following steps:

1. Identify the domain of the application that will (or does) own the D-Bus service we are interested in. For the `dnsmasq` application, this would be `dnsmasq_t`:

   `~# ps -eZ | grep dnsmasq | awk '{print $1}'`
   `system_u:system_r:dnsmasq_t:s0-s0:c0.c1023`

2. Identify the domain of the application that wants to send messages to the service. For instance, this could be the `sysadm_t` user domain.

3. Allow the two domains to interact with each other through D-Bus messages as follows:

   ```
   gen_require(`
     class dbus send_msg;
   ')
   allow sysadm_t dnsmasq_t:dbus send_msg;
   allow dnsmasq_t sysadm_t:dbus send_msg;
   ```

How it works...

When an application connects to D-Bus, the SELinux label of its connection is used as the label to check when sending messages. As there is no transition for such connections, the label of the connection is the context of the process itself (the domain); hence the selection of `dnsmasq_t` in the example.

When D-Bus receives a request to send a message to a service, D-Bus will check the SELinux policy for the `send_msg` permission. It does so by passing on the information about the session (source and target context and the permission that is requested) to the SELinux subsystem, which computes whether access should be allowed or not. The access control itself, however, is not enforced by SELinux (it only gives feedback), but by D-Bus itself as governing the message flows is solely D-Bus' responsibility.

This is also why, when developing D-Bus-related policies, both the class and permission need to be explicitly mentioned in the policy module. Without this, the development environment might error out, claiming that `dbus` is not a valid class.

D-Bus checks the context of the client that is sending a message as well as the context of the connection of the service (which are both domain labels) and see if there is a `send_msg` permission allowed. As most communication is two-fold (sending a message and then receiving a reply), the permission is checked in both directions. After all, sending a reply is just sending a message (policy-wise) in the reverse direction.

It is possible to verify this behavior with `dbus-send` if the rule is on a user domain. For instance, to look at the objects provided by the service, the D-Bus introspection can be invoked against the service:

```
~# dbus-send --system --dest=uk.org.thekelleys.dnsmasq --print-reply
/uk/org/thekelleys/dnsmasq
org.freedesktop.DBus.Introspectable.Introspect
```

When SELinux does not have the proper `send_msg` allow rules in place, the following error will be logged by D-Bus in its service logs (but no AVC denial will show up as it isn't the SELinux subsystem that denies the access):

```
Error org.freedesktop.DBus.Error.AccessDenied: An SELinux policy
prevents this sender from sending this message to this recipient. 0
matched rules; type="method_call", sender=":1.17" (uid=0 pid=6738
comm="") interface="org.freedesktop.DBus.Introspectable"
member="Introspect" error name="(unset)" requested_reply="0"
destination="uk.org.thekelleys.dnsmasq" (uid=0 pid=6635 comm="")
```

When the policy does allow the `send_msg` permission, the introspection returns an XML output showing the provided methods and interfaces for this service.

There's more...

The current D-Bus implementation is a pure user space implementation. Because more applications become dependent on D-Bus, work is being done to create a kernel-based D-Bus implementation called **kdbus**. The exact implementation details of this project are not finished yet, so it is unknown whether the SELinux access controls that are currently applicable to D-Bus will still be valid on kdbus.

Restricting service ownership

Applications that register themselves on the bus own a service name. The `uk.org.thekelleys.dnsmasq` service name is an example of this. The D-Bus policy, declared in the `busconfig` XML file at `/etc/dbus-1/system.d/` (or `session.d/` if the service is for the session bus instead of system bus) provides information for D-Bus to decide when taking ownership of a particular service is allowed.

Thanks to D-Bus' SELinux integration, additional constraints can be added to ensure that only authorized applications can take ownership of a particular service.

How to do it...

To restrict service ownership through the SELinux policy, follow the ensuing set of steps:

1. Inside the D-Bus configuration file of the service, make sure that the `own` permission is properly protected. For instance, make sure only the `root` Linux user can own the service:

```
<policy user="root">
  <allow own="uk.org.thekelleys.dnsmasq" />
</policy>
```

2. If the runtime service account can differ, it is possible to declare a `group=` parameter instead of a `user=` parameter as well.

3. Next, declare which label to associate to the service:

```
<selinux>
  <associate own="uk.org.thekelleys.dnsmasq" context="dnsmasq_t"
/>
</selinux>
```

4. In the SELinux policy, declare which domain(s) are allowed to acquire this service:

```
gen_require(`
  class dbus acquire_svc;
')
allow dnsmasq_t self:dbus acquire_svc;
```

How it works...

The D-Bus configuration allows administrators to define when service ownership for a particular service can be taken. Most services define the user (or group) that is allowed to own a service, as shown in the example. But for system services, only declaring that the Linux root user can own a particular service is definitely not sufficiently fine-grained.

Enter SELinux. With the association definition in the `busconfig` XML file, D-Bus is told that any application domain that tries to own that particular service must have the `acquire_svc` privilege (in the `dbus` class) against the mentioned context.

With this approach, administrators can ensure that other domains, even though they run as the Linux root user, are not allowed to own the service.

Although the usual approach, for the target label, is to require the context of the application itself, it is also possible to use a different context. For instance, a new type can be declared such as `dnsmasq_dbus_t` and then the SELinux policy is set to the following:

```
allow dnsmasq_t dnsmasq_dbus_t:dbus acquire_svc;
```

There's more...

The D-Bus application has a configuration file inside `/etc/selinux/mcs/contexts/`, which follows the same structure, called `dbus_contexts`. This is a default context definition for D-Bus ownership (what context should be used by default if it cannot be deduced by other means). By default, no SELinux-specific settings are provided anymore as D-Bus is now fully aware of the contexts to use, and it is not recommended to modify this file anymore.

However, it is useful to know that the file exists and is used, especially when D-Bus would be executed in a container, chroot, or other environment as D-Bus will complain if the file is missing:

```
Failed to start message bus: Failed to open
"/etc/selinux/mcs/contexts/dbus_contexts": No such file or directory
```

If the SELinux support in D-Bus needs to be disabled (but without rebuilding D-Bus), then edit `/etc/dbus-1/system.conf` and `session.conf` and remove the following line:

```
<include if_selinux_enabled="yes"
  selinux_root_relative="yes">contexts/dbus_contexts</include>
```

Understanding udev's SELinux integration

The udev device manager is responsible for handling device files inside the `/dev/` structure whenever changes occur. As many device files have different contexts, without any SELinux awareness, the udev policy would need to be enhanced with many, many named file transitions. Such a named file transition, for a device `/dev/mydevice` towards the `mydevice_t` type, would look like the following code:

```
dev_filetrans(udev_t, mydevice_t, chr_file, "mydevice")
```

However, when `/dev/mydevice1`, `/dev/mydevice2`, and so on need to be labeled as well, then each possible name would need to be iterated in the policy (named file transitions do not support regular expressions). Luckily, udev is SELinux-aware, making it unnecessary to create policy enhancements for every device file.

This recipe shows us when additional policy enhancements are needed and when not.

How to do it...

To understand how udev's SELinux integration works, the following decision criteria can be followed:

1. Whenever a device file is created by udev inside a directory with the `device_t` label, then udev will automatically label the device file with the label known to the SELinux subsystem through its `file_contexts` definitions if the target type is assigned the `device_node` attribute.

2. If the parent directory does not use the `device_t` type, then make sure that udev holds manage rights on that target type.

3. If the target file context is not associated with the `device_node` attribute, grant udev the proper `relabelto` privileges.

4. If udev's rules are configured to create symbolic links, then assert that the label of the links remains the generic `device_t` type.

How it works...

The udev application is a standard SELinux-aware application that interacts with the SELinux user space by querying the context definitions and either creating the new device files with the queried context or by relabeling the device files afterwards.

By querying the context definitions (instead of relying on the SELinux policy), administrators can easily modify the rules for different device names or include support for new device types, without the need to enhance the `udev_t` related policies. All that an administrator has to do is to configure the proper file context definition:

```
~# semanage fcontext -a -t mydevice_t -f -c /dev/mydevice[0-9]*
```

However, if the target device type (`mydevice_t`) is not associated with the `device_node` attribute, then `udev_t` will not have the privileges to relabel this device type. This attribute is vital for the support of `udev_t`, as it has relabel (and manage) rights on all device nodes through this attribute.

If a udev rule would request the creation of a device file that is not associated with the `device_node` attribute (or a different file—the requested file does not need to be a device), then an update on the SELinux policy is needed if the default context association (that is, through inheritance of the type through the parent directory) is not sufficient.

For the same reason, it is necessary to have symbolic links remain as `device_t` as the SELinux policy does not handle different types for symbolic links.

Of course, this SELinux support inside udev also has its consequences when device files are created outside of udev's handling. If that is the case, then the administrator has to make sure that the label of the files is corrected, as wrong device types can result in a system malfunction.

A popular approach for that is to relabel the entire `/dev/` structure (which is often done by a distribution `init` script to counter the default device file creation—and its default `device_t` type—from within the initial RAM filesystem or the `devtmpfs` mount):

```
~# restorecon -R /dev
```

Using cron with SELinux

Another example of an SELinux-aware application is cron. Well, actually a set of cron implementations, as there is not a single cron application. Examples of cron implementations are vixie-cron, cronie, and fcron.

The cron implementations invoke commands for (and as) a particular Linux user. As these commands are not set in stone (the main purpose of cron is to allow any command to be run for a particular user or even for the system itself), it is not possible to easily create a policy that is sufficiently fine-grained to accommodate all features provided by cron. After all, for SELinux itself, there is no difference between cron calling a command for one user or another: all that is involved is the cron domain (`crond_t`) and the target type of the command (such as `bin_t`).

For this reason, many cron implementations are made SELinux-aware, allowing the cron implementation to select the proper target context.

How to do it...

To properly interact with an SELinux-aware cron, the following steps need to be followed:

1. Make sure that the crontab files are properly labeled: `user_cron_spool_t` for the user crontabs, and `system_cron_spool_t` for the system crontab.

2. Check `/etc/selinux/mcs/contexts/default_contexts` or `/etc/selinux/mcs/contexts/users/*` for the target context of the `system_r:crond_t` domain.

3. Have the crontab file context be an entrypoint for the target domain. For instance, if the target domain for a user is its own user domain (such as `user_t`), then `user_cron_spool_t` has to be known as an entrypoint for `user_t`.

4. Set the `cron_userdomain_transition` Boolean to `on` if the target domain for user jobs is the user domain, or `off` if the target domain should be the `cronjob_t` domain.

How it works...

When cron is SELinux-aware, it is vital that it is running in the `crond_t` domain. Its internal SELinux code will query the SELinux policy to see what the target domain is for a user through the application, and if cron isn't running in the `crond_t` domain, then this query will not result in the correct set of domains:

```
~# ps -efZ | grep fcron | awk '{print $1}'
system_u:system_r:crond_t:s0-s0:c0.c1023
```

Before launching user jobs from cron, the cron application will check the file context of the user crontab file. This file context is then used to see whether the target domain for the user jobs has the user crontab file context as an entrypoint.

To know what the current target domain will be, we can use the `getseuser` helper application:

```
~# getseuser hannah system_u:system_r:crond_t:s0
seuser: user_u
Context 0    user_u:user_r:cronjob_t:s0
```

In this case, the target domain is `cronjob_t`. This should be confirmed by the `default_contexts` (or user-specific context) file:

```
~# grep crond_t /etc/selinux/mcs/contexts/users/user_u
system_r:crond_t    user_r:cronjob_t
```

If the target domain should be the user domain, then we need to toggle the right Boolean and adjust the context file accordingly:

```
~# setsebool cron_userdomain_transition on
~# grep crond_t /etc/selinux/mcs/contexts/users/user_u
system_r:crond_t    user_r:user_t
```

With the target domain known, the last thing that is needed is that the user cronjob file context is known as an entrypoint for the domain, which most cron implementations will check as a sort-of access control:

```
~# sesearch -s user_t -t user_cron_spool_t -c file -p entrypoint -A
Found 1 semantic av rules:
  allow user_t user_cron_spool_t : file entrypoint ;
```

There's more...

Not all cron implementations are SELinux-aware. If the implementation is not SELinux-aware, then the cron jobs will all run inside a single cron job container (`cronjob_t` for user cron jobs and `system_cronjob_t` for system cron jobs) with the `system_u` SELinux user and the `system_r` SELinux role.

Checking the SELinux state programmatically

If the need arises to make an SELinux-aware application, then several languages can be used. The `libselinux` package usually provides bindings for multiple programming and scripting languages. In the next set of recipes, the C programming language will be used as an example implementation.

The first step to support SELinux in an application is to check the SELinux state. In this recipe, we will show how to create an application that links with the `libselinux` library and checks the state of SELinux.

Getting ready

As we are going to update a C application, this set of recipes will assume basic knowledge of C programming. An example C application that uses all the input from this (and other) recipes can be found in the download pack of this book.

How to do it...

In order to link with `libselinux` and to check the current SELinux state, the following set of steps can be used:

1. Create a C application code file and refer to the SELinux header files through a compiler directive:

```
#ifdef SELINUX
#include <selinux/selinux.h>
#include <selinux/av_permissions.h>
#include <selinux/get_context_list.h>
#endif
```

2. In the application, have the SELinux-related function call return `success` if SELinux support should not be built-in (that is, when the compiler directive isn't set):

```
int selinux_prepare_fork(char * name) {
#ifndef SELINUX
   return 0;
#else
   ...
#endif
};
```

3. Inside the SELinux function, check whether SELinux is enabled using the `is_selinux_enabled()` function call:

```
int rc;
rc = is_selinux_enabled();
if (rc == 0) {
   ... // SELinux is not enabled
} else if (rc == -1) {
   ... // Could not check SELinux state (call failed)
} else {
   ... // SELinux is enabled
};
```

4. Add a check to see whether SELinux is in permissive or enforcing mode. Of course, this check is only needed if SELinux is enabled:

```
rc = security_getenforce();
if (rc == 0) {
   ... // SELinux is in permissive mode
} else if (rc == 1) {
   ... // SELinux is in enforcing mode
} else {
   ... // Failed to query state
};
```

5. Build the application while linking with `libselinux`:

```
~# gcc -o test -DSELINUX -lselinux test.c
```

How it works...

The `libselinux` library provides all needed functions for applications to query SELinux and interact with the SELinux subsystem. Of course, when developing applications, it remains important that SELinux support is a compile-time optional choice: not all Linux systems have SELinux enabled, so if the application is by default linked with `libselinux`, then all target systems would need to install the necessary dependencies.

But even applications that are linked with `libselinux` must be able to support systems where SELinux has been disabled; hence, the need to check the state of SELinux using `is_selinux_enabled()`.

However, this `is_selinux_enabled()` function does not return any other information (such as which policy is loaded). To check if SELinux is running in permissive mode, the call to `security_getenforce()` can be used.

A well-defined application should use this state as well to adjust its behavior: if the application is running in permissive mode, then it should try not to enforce SELinux policy-related decisions in its application logic.

To refer to the cron example from an earlier recipe: if the crontab file context is not known as an entrypoint for the selected domain, then the application should log that this is not the case, but still continue working (as the mode is set in permissive mode). Sadly, most SELinux-aware applications do not change their behavior based on the permissive state of SELinux and can still fail (or follow a different logic) as if SELinux is in the enforcing state.

There's more...

There are other similar methods available that can be used to query the SELinux state.

The `is_selinux_mls_enabled()` method, for instance, returns a value indicating whether SELinux is running with MLS or not. This is useful as some context-related methods require level information if MLS is enabled, so querying the state and changing the method calls depending on the MLS state might be necessary.

A similar function to `security_getenforce()` is `security_setenforce()`. As can be deduced from the name, this allows applications to toggle the enforcing mode of SELinux. Of course, this is only possible if the domain in which the application runs has the proper SELinux permissions.

Querying SELinux userland configuration in C

In this recipe, we will be querying the SELinux userland to obtain the default context for a given user based on the context of the current process. The process is responsible for gathering the Linux username of the user upfront.

How to do it...

Query the SELinux configuration as follows:

1. Get the current context of the process:

```
char * curcon = 0;
rc = getcon(&curcon);
if (rc) {
  ... // Getting context failed
  if (permissive) {
    ... // Continue with the application logic, ignoring
SELinux stuff
  } else {
    ... // Log failure and stop application logic
  };
};
```

2. Take the Linux username (assumed to be in the `name` variable) and get the SELinux user:

```
char * sename = 0;
char * selevel = 0;
rc = getseuserbyname(name, &sename, &selevel);
if (rc) {
  ... // Call failed. Again check permissive state
  ... // and take appropriate action.
  freecon(curcon);
};
```

3. Now, get the default context based on the obtained SELinux user (`sename`) and current context (which is handled by the method itself through the `NULL` variable):

```
char * newcon = 0;
rc = get_default_context(sename, NULL, &newcon);
if (rc) {
  ... // Call failed. Again check permissive state
  ... // and take appropriate action.
  freecon(curcon);
};
```

How it works...

In the first block, the current process context is obtained using the `getcon()` method. For the end result of this recipe, getting the current context explicitly isn't necessary—the `get_default_context()` method that is invoked later will base its decision on the current context anyway (through the second parameter, which is `NULL` in this recipe). However, having the current context known is important for logging purposes as well as to query the SELinux policy itself (as we will do in the next recipe).

The next step is to obtain the SELinux user given a Linux user. The `sename` (SELinux user) and `selevel` (SELinux sensitivity) variables are filled in by the `getseuserbyname()` method, given the Linux username (which is a regular `char *` variable).

Finally, with the SELinux user now available, `get_default_context()` is invoked to get the default context stored into the third parameter (`newcon`). If we would need to get the default context from a different context than the current one, then instead of `NULL`, the second parameter should be the context to query for:

```
rc = get_default_context(sename, curcon, &newcon);
```

There's more...

Some other methods might be interesting to use in SELinux-aware applications.

The `getprevcon()` method, for instance, returns the previous context rather than the current context of the process. This previous context is usually the context of the parent process, although with applications that can perform dynamic transitions, this can be the previous context of the current process as well.

This information can also be obtained from the `/proc/` filesystem, in the process's `attr/` subdirectory in which the `current` and `prev` files can be checked:

```
~$ id -Z
staff_u:staff_r:staff_t:s0
~$ newrole -r sysadm_r
Password:
~$ id -Z
staff_u:sysadm_r:sysadm_t:s0
~$ cat /proc/$$/attr/current
staff_u:sysadm_r:sysadm_t:s0
~$ cat /proc/$$/attr/prev
staff_u:staff_r:newrole_t:s0
```

As can be seen, after running `newrole` to switch roles, the last domain that the process was in was the `newrole_t` domain (which then performed a domain and role transition to the current context).

Applications that are allowed to perform dynamic transitions (that is, without launching new commands) can use the `setcon()` method to switch from the current context to a new context.

The `get_default_context()` method is also part of a larger family of methods. For instance, when the user has multiple roles assigned, there can be multiple contexts allowed for a particular transition. The `get_ordered_context_list()` method returns the list of contexts that are supported (whereas the `get_default_context()` method only returns the first). One can filter out specific contexts by providing the role with the `get_ordered_context_list_with_role()` method.

On MLS-enabled systems, `get_default_context_with_level()` or `get_default_context_with_rolelevel()` will apply a specified level to the resulting context as well.

Another method that is available is the `get_default_type()` method, which returns the default type for a given role. As with the other methods, this results in the SELinux code to query configuration files inside `/etc/selinux/`; in this particular case, the `default_type` file inside `/etc/selinux/mcs/contexts/`.

Interrogating the SELinux subsystem code-wise

In order to query the SELinux policy, we have seen the use of the `sesearch` command and other SELinux utilities. Code-wise, SELinux policies can be queried using the `security_compute_av_flags` method.

Getting ready

The `curcon` and `newcon` variables can be filled in through methods such as `getcon()` (for the current context) or `get_default_context()` as we have seen in the previous recipe.

How to do it...

As an example, we want to query the transition permission between two process domains. To accomplish this, the following method is used:

1. First of all, call the `security_compute_av_flags()` method:

    ```
    struct av_decision avd;
    rc = security_compute_av_flags(curcon, newcon,
      SECCLASS_PROCESS, PROCESS__TRANSITION, &avd);
    if (rc) {
      … // Method failed.
      freecon(curcon);
    ```

```
    freecon(newcon);
  };
```

2. Now read the response:

```
if (!(avd.allowed & PROCESS__TRANSITION)) {
  ... // Transition is denied
};
```

3. Check whether the current context is a permissive domain or not:

```
if (avd.flags & SELINUX_AVD_FLAGS_PERMISSIVE) {
  ... // Domain is permissive
};
```

How it works...

The `security_compute_av_flags()` method is the C method equivalent of `sesearch` (roughly speaking). It takes the source and target context, class, and permission and stores the result of the query in a specific structure (`struct av_decision`).

The class and permission entries can be obtained from the `flask.h` (for the class declarations) and the `av_permissions.h` (for the permission declarations) header files that are located inside `/usr/include/selinux/`.

The result of the query is obtained by checking whether the permission is in the decision result.

Next to the permission query, an important aspect to validate (and which is often forgotten by SELinux-aware applications) is to check whether the domain itself is marked as permissive. After all, even on an SELinux-enabled system, where SELinux is in enforcing mode, some domains can still be marked as permissive.

The `SELINUX_AVD_FLAGS_PERMISSIVE` flag is a flag added to the query response (`struct av_decision`), which allows developers to query the permissive state of domains. With this information at hand, the SELinux-aware application can still decide to continue even if the policy denies a certain activity, just as the user has requested.

There's more...

There are other methods available as well to query the SELinux policy that might be used by SELinux-aware applications.

With `selinux_check_access()`, for instance, applications can query the SELinux policy to see if a given source context has the access permission for a given class and permission on the target context. This is not the same as `security_compute_av_flags()`, as this method uses strings for the class and permission, and also has a different return based on the enforcing state of SELinux or the permissive nature of a particular domain.

Running new processes in a new context

Sometimes, it isn't possible to force a particular domain upon invocation of a new task or process. The default transition rules that can be enabled through the SELinux policy are only applicable if the source domain and file context (of the application or task to execute) are unambiguously decisive for the target context.

In applications that can run the same command (or execute commands with the same context) for different target domains, SELinux-awareness is a must.

This recipe will show how to force a particular domain for a new process.

Getting ready

The `newcon` variable that is used in this recipe can be filled in through methods such as `get_default_context()` as we have seen in a previous recipe.

How to do it...

To launch a process in a specific context, go through the following steps:

1. Tell SELinux what the new context should be:

```
int rc = setexeccon(newcon);
if (rc) {
  ... // Call failed
  freecon(newcon);
};
```

2. Fork and execute the command. For instance, to execute `id -Z`, the following code is used:

```
pid_t child;
child = fork();
if (child < 0) {
  ... // Fork failed
} else if (child == 0) {
  int pidrc;
  pidrc = execl("/usr/bin/id", "id", "-Z", NULL);
  if (pidrc != 0) {
    ... // Command failed
  };
} else {
  ... // Parent process
  int status;
  wait(&status);
};
```

How it works...

Applications that want newly executed tasks to run in a particular context need to tell the SELinux subsystem that the next `execve`, `execl`, or other `exec*` method should result in the child process running in the new domain.

Of course, the SELinux policy must still allow the transition policy-wise, even though there is no more need for an automatic domain transition in the policy (as this would require an unambiguous decision, which is exactly what isn't possible if the source domain and file context are the same for different target contexts):

```
allow crond_t self : process setexec;
allow crond_t staff_t : process transition;
```

The `setexec` permission allows the source domain to explicitly tell the SELinux subsystem what context the task should run in. Without this permission, the call to `setexeccon()` would fail.

There's more...

The `setexeccon()` method has a sibling method called `getexeccon()`. This method returns the context that would be assigned when executing a new process (which would provide a validation of the last `setexeccon()` call).

Another similar method is the `setexecfilecon()` method. This method allows SELinux-aware applications to take the SELinux policy decisions into account in case of file-based transition information. So, if there is a domain transition known when executing a particular file, then this domain transition is honored. If not, the fallback type provided through the `setexecfilecon()` method is used:

```
char * fallbackcon =
  "system_u:object_r:openscap_helper_script_t:s0";
char * filename = "/usr/libexec/openscap/probe_process";
...
rc = setexecfilecon(filename, fallbackcon);
```

In this example, if the context of the `probe_process` file is used in the SELinux policy to create an automatic domain transition upon invocation by the current application, then that target domain is used for the application execution. However, if the context of the `probe_process` file is the one that does not trigger any automatic domain transition, then the `fallbackcon` context is used for the next application execution.

Reading the context of a resource

It is, of course, also important to obtain the context of a resource if the application is SELinux-aware. This could be for logging purposes or to decide which domain to transition to (based on the resource context, current context, username, and so on).

How to do it...

To read the context of a resource, the following methods are available:

1. Given a file path, the following call to `getfilecon()` will provide the context of the file:

    ```
    security_context_t filecon = 0;
    char * path = "/etc/passwd";
    rc = getfilecon(path, &filecon);
    if (rc < 0) {
      ... // Call failed
    };
    ... // Do stuff with the context
    freecon(filecon);
    ```

2. To get the context of a process, assuming the `pid` variable (of the `pid_t` type) has the proper process ID in it, the following code is used:

    ```
    security_context_t pidcon = 0;
    rc = getpidcon(pid, &pidcon);
    if (rc < 0) {
      ... // Call failed
    };
    ... // Do stuff with the context
    freecon(pidcon);
    ```

How it works...

The SELinux library has various methods for obtaining the contexts of resources. File and process types are shown in the recipe, but other methods exist as well. For instance, with the `fgetfilecon()` method, the context of a file descriptor can be obtained. All these methods provide the context in a standard string (`char *`) format.

After getting the context of a resource, it is important to free the context when it is no longer used. Otherwise, a memory leak will occur in the application as there are no other methods that will clean up the contexts.

There's more...

When labeled networking is used (for instance, with CIPSO/NetLabel support or labeled IPSec), then the `getpeercon()` method can be used to obtain the context of the peer that participates in the communication session.

Alongside querying the context, it is also possible to tell the SELinux subsystem that file creation should result in that file being created immediately with a particular context. For this, the `setfscreatecon()` method can be used—this is also the method that recent udev versions use when creating new device files in `/dev/`.

Index

Thank you for buying
SELinux Cookbook

About Packt Publishing

Packt, pronounced 'packed', published its first book "*Mastering phpMyAdmin for Effective MySQL Management*" in April 2004 and subsequently continued to specialize in publishing highly focused books on specific technologies and solutions.

Our books and publications share the experiences of your fellow IT professionals in adapting and customizing today's systems, applications, and frameworks. Our solution based books give you the knowledge and power to customize the software and technologies you're using to get the job done. Packt books are more specific and less general than the IT books you have seen in the past. Our unique business model allows us to bring you more focused information, giving you more of what you need to know, and less of what you don't.

Packt is a modern, yet unique publishing company, which focuses on producing quality, cutting-edge books for communities of developers, administrators, and newbies alike. For more information, please visit our website: www.packtpub.com.

About Packt Open Source

In 2010, Packt launched two new brands, Packt Open Source and Packt Enterprise, in order to continue its focus on specialization. This book is part of the Packt Open Source brand, home to books published on software built around Open Source licenses, and offering information to anybody from advanced developers to budding web designers. The Open Source brand also runs Packt's Open Source Royalty Scheme, by which Packt gives a royalty to each Open Source project about whose software a book is sold.

Writing for Packt

We welcome all inquiries from people who are interested in authoring. Book proposals should be sent to author@packtpub.com. If your book idea is still at an early stage and you would like to discuss it first before writing a formal book proposal, contact us; one of our commissioning editors will get in touch with you.

We're not just looking for published authors; if you have strong technical skills but no writing experience, our experienced editors can help you develop a writing career, or simply get some additional reward for your expertise.

SELinux System Administration

ISBN: 978-1-78328-317-0   Paperback: 120 pages

A comprehensive guide to walk you through SELinux access controls

1. Use SELinux to further control network communications.

2. Enhance your system's security through SELinux access controls.

3. Set up SELinux roles and users as well as their sensitivity levels.

Embedded Linux Development with Yocto Project

ISBN: 978-1-78328-233-3   Paperback: 142 pages

Develop fascinating Linux-based projects using the groundbreaking Yocto Project tools

1. Optimize Yocto Project's capabilities to develop captivating embedded Linux projects.

2. Facilitates efficient system development by helping you avoid known pitfalls.

3. Demonstrates concepts in a practical and easy-to-understand way.

Please check **www.PacktPub.com** for information on our titles

Linux Mint Essentials

ISBN: 978-1-78216-815-7   Paperback: 324 pages

A practical guide to Linux Mint for the novice to the professional

1. Learn to use Linux Mint like a pro, starting with the installation and going all the way through maintaining your system.

2. Covers everything you need to know in order to be productive, including browsing the Internet, creating documents, and installing software.

3. Hands-on activities reinforce your knowledge.

Mastering Kali Linux for Advanced Penetration Testing

ISBN: 978-1-78216-312-1   Paperback: 356 pages

A practical guide to testing your network's security with Kali Linux, the preferred choice of penetration testers and hackers

1. Conduct realistic and effective security tests on your network.

2. Demonstrate how key data systems are stealthily exploited, and learn how to identify attacks against your own systems.

3. Use hands-on techniques to take advantage of Kali Linux, the open source framework of security tools.

Please check **www.PacktPub.com** for information on our titles